selected works
achim wollscheid

Achim Wollscheid
selected works

impressum   **ISBN 3-943801-01-3**
Copyright 2001

produced and designed by Charly Steiger

printed by Vier-Türme-GmbH
Münsterschwarzach

SELEKTION SB 04
Hohenstaufenstrasse 8, 60327 Frankfurt a.M.
www.selektion.com

Supported by „Hessisches Ministerium für Wissenschaft und Kunst"
Gefördert mit Mitteln des Hessischen Ministeriums für Wissenschaft
und Kunst.

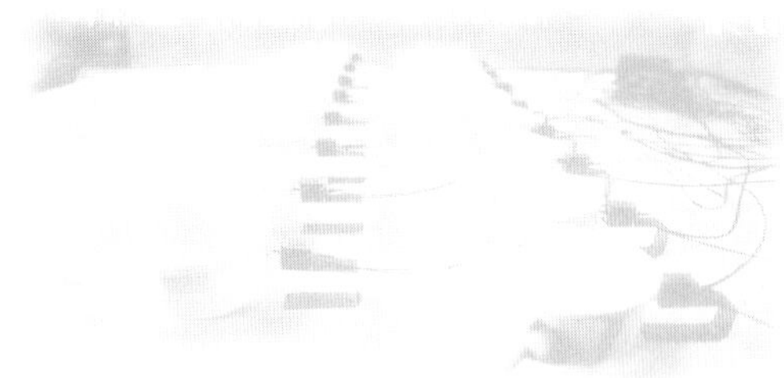

selected works

achim wollscheid

inhalt

To write a text for his own catalogue may seduce the artist: to supplement the omitted, to state the in-evident, to assert consistency to the visually fragmentary, and to generally give a closed, well-shaped description, referring to illustrations a meaning whose lack of evidence in comparison to the actual event can be sensed. In short: to tell what it's all about...
This is specifically seductive in the case of multi-media art or of the general art whose media cannot be depicted: sound, movement and

performative orders

achim wollscheid

interactive systems. Because of the fact that something essential, namely the experience of correlation fanned out by such works, evades depiction, calls for the use of words, which is still unable to bring back the passed-by but aids in conveying a concise understanding.

If in this catalogue short comments are added to the illustrations it occurs for two reasons: on the one hand, indeed in the sense of an explanation, I would like to name some of the social, technical and artistical aspects which make up the work and its embeddedness into context (which adjoined by further information could result in some kind of "image"). On the other hand, these texts oppose the exclusive and exposed character of the illustration suggesting autonomy: because this work is necessarily inserted into a net of social and technical conditions —— and this is done not unwillingly but with intention.

Being thus related, embedded (and oriented toward a "public sphere") it differentiates itself from works which attempt to reach autonomy through context-asceticism: it is unimaginable and unfeasible without a material, without a practical connection to a previously existing context. This conscious deliverance, this affirmation to the existing, may contain the wish to save a bit of autonomy by abandoning the "object": autonomy here is understood as a transformation within a realm of interaction caused by the artistic implant, which understands reality as one of many possible forms.

Having said this about intentions I succumb to the seduction to name one aspect which I believe can function as a guide to this work: order and its per- or trans-formance. All orders, be it the so-called natural or social, from those of the animal kingdom to those of traffic or clothing, are projections —— matters of opinion shared by a more or less numerous amount of people. And these opinions serve their own execution: as the collective choreography in the variety of concreteness.

My interest does not directly concern the different manifestations, but rather the rules which govern their practical execution and chanelling: rules which are often stored in technical devices to state, prolong, deviate or illustrate such orders. The term transformation I take as a metaphor for activities which implant changes into these manifestations, be it technical or social (such as computer-generated light-systems or singing in choir formations): systems which cause shifts or deviations on the systematics of order.

The medium of such an artistic implant is secondary and oriented toward the medium of the respective context: light, where light as an ordering factor directs movement in space, sound, where it has a key-function in a social-spectrum or abstract signs, where graphical patterns organize space. Opinion is therefore not the artistic work, but the onlooker's or participant's feedback, which the work itself instigates as a function.

achim wollscheid

Einen Text zu seinem eigenen Katalog zu schreiben mag den Künstler verführen: dazu, Ausgelassenes zu ergänzen, Nicht-Ersichtliches zu behaupten, dem visuell Fragmentarischen konzeptuelle Konsistenz zuzuschreiben, überhaupt dem Abgebildeten, das den Mangel an Ersichtlichkeit im Vergleich zum Stattgefundenen immer wieder erahnen läßt, einen Sinn zu geben, der einen irgendwie abgerundeten, verweiskräftigen, in sich geschlossenen Zusammenhang behauptet. Eben schließlich doch zu sagen, worum es geht...

Dies ist im Fall multi-medialer Kunst, oder solcher, die sich der Abbildung entziehender Mittel verwendet: Klang, Bewegung, interaktive Systeme, besonders verführerisch. Denn die Tatsache, daß ein Essentielles, nämlich das Erleben der Zusammenhänge, die solche Arbeiten auffächern, sich der Abbildung weitgehend entzieht, ruft geradezu nach Worten, die, wenn sie auch das Unwiederbringliche nicht herbeizaubern, so doch immerhin ein übersichtliches Verstehen ermöglichen sollen.

Wenn nun hier im Katalog tatsächlich den Abbildungen kurze Erläuterungen beigefügt sind, geschieht dies aus zwei Gründen. Einerseits möchte ich, durchaus im Sinne des Erklärens, einige der sozialen, technischen und künstlerischen Aspekte nennen, die die Arbeit und ihre jeweilige Einbettung im Kontext ausmachten (was zumindest im Anschluß an andere Informationen etwas wie eine „Vorstellung" ergeben kann), andererseits sollen die kurzen Texte den freistellenden, Autonomie suggerierenden Charakter der Abbildung konterkarieren; denn diese Arbeit ist notwendig eingefügt in ein Netz von Bedingungen sozialer und technischer Art – und sie ist dies keineswegs unfreiwillig, sondern beabsichtigterweise.

In dieser Bezugnahme, in dieser Einbettung (und in ihrer Hinwendung zum „Öffentlichen") unterscheidet sie sich von Arbeiten, die Autonomie im Sinne einer Kontext-Askese zu erreichen suchen: sie ist ohne ein Ausgangsmaterial, ohne einen handgreiflich praktischen Anschluß an vorgängig Vorhandenes nicht machbar und nicht vorstellbar. In dieser bewußten Auslieferung, in der Affirmation an das Gegebene, liegt vielleicht der Wunsch, auch durch die Preisgabe des „objekthaften" solcher Arbeit ein Stück Autonomie zu retten: Autonomie als verstehende, transformierende Etablierung eines Interaktionsbereichs, in dem – durch den künstlerischen Eingriff – Realität als eine Form des Möglichen neben anderen denkbar wird.

Wenn nun schon soviel zur Absicht gesagt ist, möchte ich der Verführung nachgeben und einen Aspekt nennen, von dem ich glaube, daß er als Hinführung zur Arbeit dienen kann: den methodischen der Ordnung und ihrer Per- oder Trans-formation.

Alle Ordnungen, seien es die sogenannt natürlichen oder die sozialen, von der des Tierreichs bis zu der des Straßenverkehrs oder der Kleidung sind Projektionen, von einer mehr oder weniger umfangreichen Menge an Personen geteilte Ansichtssachen. Wobei diese Sicht der Dinge auch gleichzeitig ihrer Bewältigung dient – der gemeinschaftlichen Choreographie in der Vielfalt der Gegenständlichkeiten.

Mein Blick fällt nun nicht direkt auf die Äußerungsformen, sondern vielmehr auf die Regeln, die ihre praktische Bewältigung, ihre Kanalisierung gewährleisten; Regeln, die sehr oft in technischen Vorrichtungen gespeichert sind und solche Ordnungen behaupten, verstärken, verlängern, umleiten oder auch nur illustrieren. Unter dem Begriff Transformation verstehe ich nun solche Vorgehensweisen, die in die Manifestationen solcher Ordnungen, seien sie technischer oder sozialer Art (z.B. computergesteuerte Licht-Schaltungen oder Singen in chorischen Formen), Umstellungen einbringen: Systeme, die in der Systematik der Ordnungen Verschiebungen oder Abweichungen hervorrufen.

Das Medium des künstlerischen Implantats ist dabei sekundär und orientiert sich an der Medialität des Kontexts: Licht, wo Licht als Ordnungsfaktor Raum oder Bewegung bestimmt, Klang, wo er in der sozialen Organisation Schlüsselfunktion hat, oder abstrakte Zeichen, wo graphische Ordnungen Raum organisieren.

Ansichtssache ist demnach nicht die künstlerische Arbeit, sondern das Feedback des Betrachters/Teilnehmers, das sie als Funktion hervorruft.

spatial interference

beatrice von bismarck

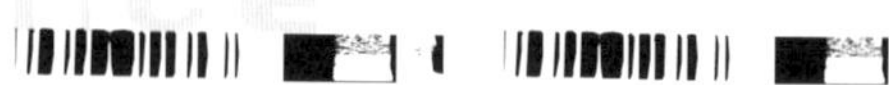

a place designed by city-planning is transformed into a space by the movements of the pedestrians, a space, says de Certeau, can be described as a place in which performative action takes place. He specifies this definition with reference to the speech-act comparing space to the uttered word, which changes according to the transformations caused by the succession of contexts.

Those who like de Certeau regard narration as a work-process, whose course constantly and interminably transforms places into spaces and spaces into places, can imagine this process also extended to the realms of the visual and the acoustical. The flexible frame of reference, which constitutes a place as a space, is expanded by additional reference-systems. The passers-by who use the space while entering and crossing it, find themselves, in addition to the demands and tasks which previously motivated their actions, exposed to new contexts generated by sound and light. Movements of the body proceed into a continuously changing relationship to the movements of light, sound and, again, other bodies. Contingent, if not constantly threatened by dissolution, the one pattern of movement melts into the other, opens and forms anew. "Re-recorded, cut-up, re-recorded" –– is the "off" description of a transformation-process in one of A. Wollscheid's works, in the course of which the specificity of movements becomes blurred to make space for others. Interplays between the aesthetical and the social. Not a superimposition of structures, where the bottom layer will always shine through the upper, no palimpsest, but a succession of refractions, whose fragments join to form a spatial construct made out of miniature parts.

A space emerges, which defuses the conditions of the environmental space; an interference with the existing structure of the place. The degree of autonomy is set according to the interactive potential of those using the space, be it passive or active –– the action of the users is part of the transformation-processes. The action can be a necessary and planned, though subconscious and unprepared deliverer of impulses for mediatized reaction, but it can also co-operate in the shaping of such reaction, create input in the course of translations between the realm of the visual and the acoustical. However, what is fixed is the scope of action. The space presupposes its users as a condition for its constitution, whereas the users receive their task in dependence on the space's existence.

Still there remains the option for the user to simultaneously assume the role of the observer as well as the observed. Because for each space there exists an outer space, from which it can be observed, where the

transformation-processes can be followed, from where it becomes a stage. The separating line between stage and audience as spaces of different experiences is drawn to be crossed. The first potentially accidental crossing into the playing area becomes, with each new attempt, a readiness, to willingly expose oneself to a transformation of

the conventions of activity and experience, to escape the threat of their entropic dissolution, to orient oneself in a different network of relations.

The experiment presupposes a third space, which exceeds stage and audience. Not only the design of the playing area is conceived in it, such as in city-planning, but also the direction which decides the inter-relation of the different movable elements: sensual stimuli, actions of the users and the changing structures of the emerging spaces. The input of outside elements into the spaces constituted by different frams also occurs here. Space and person of the planner are exempted from this interaction. They participate through their effects, without exposure. Parti-cipatory involvement becomes reconstructable only from a viewpoint where the processes of direction, observation and action again emerge as a space whose changing relations are structured by a search for the limits and potentials of distances.

In seiner „Kunst des Handelns" nahm Michel de Certeau 1988 eine Unterscheidung zwischen Ort und Raum vor. Nach ihr ist der Raum definiert über eine Menge beweglicher Elemente und ihr Verhältnis zu einander. So wie erst die Fußgänger den von der Stadtplanung entworfenen Ort durch ihre Bewegungen in einen Raum verwandeln, läßt sich für ihn ein Raum allgemein als ein Ort beschreiben, mit dem man etwas macht. Im Verweis auf den Sprechakt präzisiert er diese Begriffsbestimmung weiter, indem er den Raum einem ausgesprochenen Wort gleichsetzt, das sich durch die Transformationen, die sich aus den aufeinanderfolgenden Kontexten ergeben, verändert.

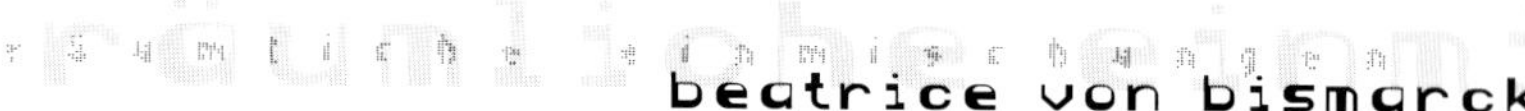

beatrice von bismarck

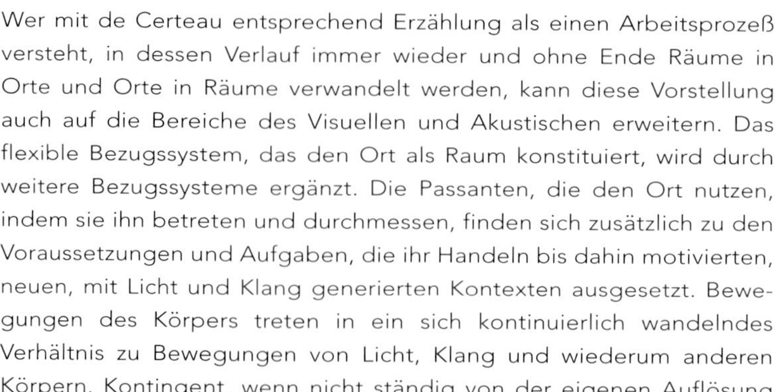

Wer mit de Certeau entsprechend Erzählung als einen Arbeitsprozeß versteht, in dessen Verlauf immer wieder und ohne Ende Räume in Orte und Orte in Räume verwandelt werden, kann diese Vorstellung auch auf die Bereiche des Visuellen und Akustischen erweitern. Das flexible Bezugssystem, das den Ort als Raum konstituiert, wird durch weitere Bezugssysteme ergänzt. Die Passanten, die den Ort nutzen, indem sie ihn betreten und durchmessen, finden sich zusätzlich zu den Voraussetzungen und Aufgaben, die ihr Handeln bis dahin motivierten, neuen, mit Licht und Klang generierten Kontexten ausgesetzt. Bewegungen des Körpers treten in ein sich kontinuierlich wandelndes Verhältnis zu Bewegungen von Licht, Klang und wiederum anderen Körpern. Kontingent, wenn nicht ständig von der eigenen Auflösung

bedroht, gehen die einen Bewegungsmuster in andere über, in ihnen auf und formieren sich neu. „Re-recorded, cut-up, re-recorded" umreißt Achim Wollscheid aus dem off einen Transformationsprozess, in dessen Verlauf die Spezifika von Bewegungsabläufen undeutlich werden, um anderen zu weichen. Wechselspiele zwischen Ästhetischem und Sozialem. Nicht Überlagerung von Strukturen, deren oberste immer noch die unterste durchscheinen läßt, kein Palimpsest, sondern eine Aufeinanderfolge von Brechungen, deren Bruchstücke sich zu einem kleinstteiligen räumlichen Gebilde zusammensetzen.

Es entsteht ein Raum, der die Bedingungen des ihn umgebenden

Raumes außer Kraft setzt. Eine Einmischung in das bestehende Gefüge
der Orte. Der Grad der Eigengesetzlichkeit richtet sich nach dem
jeweiligen interaktiven Handlungspotential der den Raum Nutzenden.
Mal passiver, mal aktiver ist die Handlung der Nutzenden an den
Transformationsprozessen beteiligt. Sie kann einmal notwendiger und
eingeplanter, dennoch unbewußter und unvorbereiteter Impulsgeber
sein für medial transportierte Reaktion; sie kann aber auch an der
Gestaltung solcher Reaktionen mitarbeiten, sich ihrerseits einmischen,
nun in der Abfolge von Übersetzungen zwischen dem Bereich des
Visuellen und des Akustischen. Das Handlungsspektrum jedoch ist
festgelegt. Der Raum sieht die ihn Nutzenden als Voraussetzung seiner
eigenen Konstituierung vor, die Nutzenden erhalten ihre Aufgabe in

Abhängigkeit von der Existenz des Raumes.

Immer bleibt ihnen jedoch die Möglichkeit, sich zugleich sowohl in der
Rolle des Betrachteten als auch der Betrachtenden wieder zu finden.
Denn für jeden der Räume gibt es einen Raum außerhalb, von dem aus
er angesehen werden kann, von dem aus die Transformationsprozesse
verfolgt werden können, von dem aus er zur Bühne wird. Die Grenze
zwischen Bühnen- und Zuschauerraum als zwei unterschiedlichen
Erfahrungsräumen, ist darauf angelegt, überschritten zu werden.
Der möglicherweise zufällige erste Übertritt in das Spielfeld hinein
gestaltet sich mit jedem weiteren Mal als Bereitschaft, sich mut-
willig der Umformung von Handlungs- und Erfahrungskonventionen
auszusetzen, sich dem Versuch ihrer scheinbar entropischen Auflösung
zu unterziehen, um sich in einem anderen Bezugsgewebe wieder-
zufinden.

Die Versuchsanordnung setzt einen dritten Raum voraus, der über
diejenigen, die Bühne und Auditorium bilden, hinausreicht. Von hier
aus erfolgt nicht nur das Design der Spielfläche, wie etwa in der Städte-
planung, sondern auch die Regieanweisung, die über das Verhältnis
der verschiedenen Bewegungselemente zueinander bestimmt: der
Sinnesreize, der Handlungen der Akteure sowie der sich wandelnden
Strukturen der geschaffenen Räume. Von hier aus erfolgt die Einmischung der Fremdelemente in die durch unterschiedliche Rahmungen
gegebenen Räume. Raum und Person des Planenden jedoch
bleiben von den Interaktionen ausgenommen, sie nehmen an
den Interferenz-Prozessen indirekt, durch ihre Wirkung teil,
ohne ihnen ausgesetzt zu sein. Die beteiligte Einbindung
erschließt sich erst aus einer Warte, von der aus sich die
Vorgänge von Regie, Betrachtung und Mitspielen wiederum als
Raum formieren, deren wandelbare Verhältnisse maßgeblich
durch Fragen nach Grenzen und Möglichkeiten von Distanzen
strukturiert sind.

"2 rot" - an attempt to remember

"2 rot" moves Achim Wollscheid's work into the context of theater.
Outside of the closed frame of fictional attempts to imitate reality the
"performance-project without an author" evolves into the mechanical

transformance in sound-body-systems

kattrin deufert

function of theater as mnemonic work for bodies. Human bodies,
moving in public space "automatically" develop mnemonic spaces.
"2 rot" addresses both individual and collective memory, where the
seemingly natural presence of the human body not only becomes an
object for memory, but in which this memory is also acted out against

the representational simulation in theatrical bodies.

In the sense of the mechanics of theater "2 rot" can be thought of as contextual
and site-specific –– an open project between performance and installation.
In the first performance of "rot", presented as part of the 1994 Trierer Kultur-
sommer a performance space evolves amoungst the players according to the
possible formal principles of a dialogical structure which is not pre-structured
through delivered, rehearsed and repeatable information. In analogy to Wollscheid's computer-controlled sound- and light-systems the "Gestalt" of the bodily
impulses in sound, language and movement emerges during performance
through the mechanics of interaction. For the actors the experiment consists in
isolating different physical and language-related means of communication and
using them in their formal function –– reduced from any specific content. During
rehearsal, modes of communication are studied, which during performance ––
in real-time –– differentiate text and movement. A physical impulse is given,
recognized as information, translated into the next impulse and emitted. A
human "communication-machine" without memory is at work, which, in spite of
occurring mistakes in translation, could potentially continue ad infinitum.
Such a system, which more or less automatically generates the performers'
translation of language into sound, of facial expression into gesture, facilitates
the creation of complex action through any chosen impulse at any place and

any time. "rot" thus becomes kind of an "écriture automatique" of a
functional body-system, that tries to say goodbye to memory.

Like any machine, this one is also susceptible to disturbance. Methods
are consciously unfeasible; modes of dependency which provoke the

system's demolition are established between the actors. The change from system to chaos and back to system is "pre-programmed". "2 rot" continues. In its Frankfurt performance-space the changeabilty of a collective mechanism of the body is instigated through internal dynamic changes or through external impulses of the technical sound and light-installation. New modes of simultaneous communication and transformation of speech and movement must independently be deduced from the momentary state of the game. The rules for "2 rot" are trained by the performers in order to increase the flexibility and playability of the whole as a communicating system: for a short time the "machine" is reignited, accelerated until –– after a phase of directed chaos –– it decomposes into its individual parts to finish as their monadic self-expression. Juxtaposed to this process is the action of a second

group –– remotely reminiscent of the structures of a drama, which was rehearsed independently but conceptually linked to the experiment of the first. The "machine", which permanently produces speech and movement under pressure of the system, is juxtaposed by three variations of a process, in which the speech and movement of the four players are the media for an attempt to remember. A story imagined or remembered during rehearsal is constantly retold and transformed under changing conditions. Memory requires repetition and variation. Only in one passage of the performance is "the" story –– which is constantly transformed through translations and spatial fanning out of the narration –– is softly retold as a construction of wholeness.

The continual decomposition of a communication-machine without memory is thus opposed by variations of human memory. Anybody sharing in this form of theater can experience the process of remembering the forgotten, whereby nothing specific is recalled, and anybody can witness the process of a creation of contents, which nevertheless does not connote anything specific. The co-presence of menmosyne and mechanics of the body in "2 rot" becomes a mutual challenge incorporating the audience. Complex actions, which create and are created by the performance, become present as virtual. Repeatable and infinitely volatile these actions can be like they are, they can be different or they may not be at all. A secured mechanism of representation is exchanged for a mode of uncertainty, which moves the audience into the real realm of its own risk. We share the process of remembrance, but not memory, like interruptions through a sudden irritation –– but everybody gets frightened at a different moment.

In the course of the technical sounds, of the voices and of the light, all participants share one common space of experience. Theater as a shared

situation becomes present in "2 rot" not as the perception of different expressions of presence, but as a growing consciousness of presence in the sense of a co-presence in the real. But at any time a sudden change can happen, which irritates that which was intimate just before and cancels the consciousness of presence.

kattrin deufert

„2 rot" – ein Erinnerungsversuch

„2 rot" rückt Achim Wollscheids künstlerische Arbeit in den Kontext von Theater. Außerhalb des geschlossenen Rahmens fiktiver Nachahmungsversuche im Realen bewegt das Performance-Projekt ohne Autor sich in der mechanischen Funktion von Theater als Gedächtnisarbeit für Körper. Menschliche Körper, die sich in öffentlichen Räumen bewegen, bilden ,automatisch' Gedächtnis-Orte aus. „2 rot" thematisiert sowohl eine individuelle als auch kollektive Gedächtnisarbeit, indem die natürlich scheinende Präsenz des menschlichen Körpers nicht nur zum Gegenstand von Erinnerung, sondern diese gegen ein abbildhaft Simuliertes von Theaterkörpern ausgespielt wird.

„2 rot" läßt sich im Sinne einer Theatermechanik kontext- und ortsspezifisch denken – als ein offenes Projekt zwischen Performance und Installation.

Für den ersten Versuch „rot", der während des Trierer Kultursommers 1994 gezeigt wurde, entsteht nach möglichen formalen Prinzipien einer dialogischen Struktur unter den Spielern ein Aufführungsraum, der durch keine im voraus bereitgestellte, erprobte und wiederholbare Information gespeist ist. Analog zu Wollscheids computergesteuerten Klang- und Lichtsystemen, bildet sich die Gestalt der körperlichen Laut-, Sprach- und Bewegungsimpulse über die Mechanik des Zusammenspiels erst in der Zeit der Aufführung aus. Das Experiment für die Spieler bestand darin, unterschiedliche körperliche und sprachliche Mittel der Kommunikation zu isolieren und auf deren formale, d.h. von spezifischen Inhalten unabhängige Funktion reduziert, zu gebrauchen. Während der Proben werden Kommunikationsregeln einstudiert, mithilfe derer in einer Aufführung – in Echtzeit – Texte und Bewegungen auseinander entwickelt werden.

Ein Körperimpuls wird gesetzt, als Information erkannt und in einen neuen Impuls übersetzt und weitergeleitet. Eine erinnerungslose menschliche ‚Kommunikations-Maschine‘ kommt ins Laufen, die – trotz auftretender Übersetzungsfehler – potentiell unendlich lange weiterarbeiten könnte.

Ein solches System, das mehr oder weniger automatisch den Übersetzungsvorgang von Sprache in Klang, Mimik und Körperbewegung zwischen den Performern steuert, ermöglicht es, durch einen beliebig gewählten Impuls an jedem Ort und zu jeder Zeit im Raum komplexe Spielvorgänge in Gang zu setzen. „rot" wurde so zu einer Art räumlicher „écriture automatique" eines funktionalen Körpersystems, das sich von einem Gedächtnis zu verabschieden versuchte.

Wie jede Maschine ist auch diese störanfällig. Regeln sind bewußt unerfüllbar; zwischen den Spielerinnen sind Abhängigkeitsverhältnisse etabliert, die den Ausstieg, die Sprengung des Systems provozieren. Der Wechsel vom System zum Chaos zum System ... ist ‚vor-programmiert‘.

„2 rot" geht weiter. In dem Frankfurter Aufführungsraum wird die Veränderlichkeit einer kollektiven Körpermechanik durch systeminterne dynamische Wechsel oder durch externe Impulse der technischen Klang- und Lichtinstallation benutzt, so, daß neue systemfremde Formen der gleichzeitigen Kommunikation und Transformation von Sprache und Bewegung aus dem Moment, in dem das Spiel sich gerade befindet, selbst herausgefunden werden müssen. Für „2 rot" werden zudem die Regeln von den Performern so trainiert, daß sie als kommunikatives System die Beweglichkeit und Spielmöglichkeit des Ganzen vergrößern: für eine kurze Zeit wird die Maschine erneut angeworfen, beschleunigt, bis sie nach einer Phase des gesteuerten Chaos in ihre Einzelteile zerfällt und in deren monadischem Selbstausdruck endet.

Kontrapunktisch verflochten mit diesem – von Ferne an die Strukturen des Dramas erinnernden – Prozeß ist das Spiel einer zweiten Gruppe, das zwar unabhängig geprobt wurde, konzeptionell aber eng an den Versuch der ersten gebunden ist. Der ‚Maschine‘, die unter Systemzwang ständig neu Sprache und Bewegung hervorbringt, werden hier

drei Variationen eines Prozesses gegenübergestellt, in der Sprache und Bewegung von vier weiteren Spielerinnen Medien eines Erinnerungsversuches sind. Eine während der Proben erfundene / erinnerte Geschichte wird immer wieder neu und unter veränderten Bedingungen erzählt und dadurch verwandelt. Erinnerung braucht Wiederholung und Variation. Nur in einer Phase der Aufführung wird ‚die' Geschichte, die immer wieder neu durch räumliche Bewe-

gung im Erzählvorgang und durch Übersetzungsprozesse transformiert wird, als Konstruktion von Ganzheit leise hörbar.

Dem allmählichen Zerfall einer gedächtnislosen Kommunikationsmaschine werden also Variationen menschlichen Erinnerns gegenübergestellt. Jeder, der die Situation dieser Form von Theater teilt, hat für sich die Möglichkeit, den Prozeß von Erinnerung an Vergessenes zu erleben, ohne daß an etwas Bestimmtes erinnert werden soll, und gleichzeitig dem Prozeß der Entstehung von Bedeutung beizuwohnen, der nichts Bestimmtes zu bedeuten

hat. Die Kopräsenz von Gedächtnisarbeit und Körpermechanik wird in „2 rot" zur wechselseitigen Herausforderung, die das Publikum miteinbezieht.
Komplexe Spielvorgänge, die sich in der und durch die Aufführungssituation bestimmen, werden als virtuelle präsent. Wiederholt und unabschließbar sich entziehend, können diese so, aber auch ganz anders oder gar nicht sein. Ein gesicherter Repräsentations-Mechanismus wird abgelöst von einem Modus der Unbestimmtheit, der das Publikum in ein reales Feld des eigenen Risikos verschiebt. Was wir teilen, ist der Prozeß des Erinnerns, nicht die Erinnerungen selbst, sowie Momente der Unterbrechung durch eine plötzliche Irritation, aber jeder erschrickt an einer anderen Stelle.
Im Spiel der technischen Sounds, der Körper-Stimmen und des Lichtes entsteht allen beteiligten ein Erfahrungsraum. Theater als gemeinsam geteilte Situation stellt sich in „2 rot" nicht so sehr über die Wahrnehmung unterschiedlichster Ausdrucksformen von Präsenz, als durch ein wachsendes Bewußtsein von Präsenz im Sinne einer Kopräsenz im Realen ein. Jederzeit kann sich plötzlich eine Veränderung einstellen, die als Moment der Irritation des gerade noch Vertrauten das Bewußtsein von Präsenz widerruft.

Fluids

When Duchamp presented a urinal at the first exhibition of the Society of Independent Artists in 1917, called it Fountain and signed it "R. Mutt" he not only challenged notions of the art-object, disarming a

history of object-making based upon technical skill, genius and the artist's touch; in this gesture he also brought into question what it meant to be an artist. The role of the artist takes a dramatic shift following the Duchampian moment. The appearance of the ready-made Fountain coincides with, if not helps initiate, the appearance of a Modern avant-garde and its radical redefining of cultural paradigms. As the theorist Alice Jardine observes, a society enters modernism when it begins to question the very representations it makes of itself. With Fountain the art object is destabilized, made uneasy. This

destabilization in turn throws into question the nature of artistic production in general. In contrast to preceding notions of the role of the artist within society, the Modern artist is cast as an adversary to the status quo –– Duchamp himself disguised his work in order to "test" his peers who were organizing the exhibition and their commitment to its not being juried. (It is interesting to note that Fountain was deemed unacceptable for exhibition.)

The Duchamp urinal throws art into a reexamination of itself by challenging it as an autonomous object without consequence, and in turn, prompting the artist into self-examination. The question of the role of the artist appears as a theoretical thread throughout the century, informing developments in the avant-garde, from the Bauhaus' coupling of art and engineering, Pop Art and the Warholian production line of glamour, Conceptualism's' dematerialization of the object and the emergence of "artist as philosopher", to Beuys' Free University, social sculpture and the politics of education––here, artist as "policy maker". This shift in ethos fosters a critical stance toward established conventions and proposes that art act as both critique and progenitor of culture. Further, it aims to challenge existing conventions of the status of the object in itself, as a tautology, and in contrast supports artistic production that acts as a catalyst for discourse. From here the artist in essence takes up the position of the lost object, one whose very subject-hood signifies independence, free-thinking, critical examination –– in essence, artist as agent.

Bodies

The work of artist Achim Wollscheid follows this lineage, proposing relationships between art and public space that bring into question the role of the artist today and the function of art in general. Working from the early 80's to the present, Frankfurt-based Wollscheid has produced a compelling body of work whose concern for sound, light, space and interactivity opens onto and engages with aesthetic and social issues. Indicative of Wollscheid's approach is a commitment to site-specificity. In his work the art object is reduced to a systematic response to a given situation: light panels react to passers-by, sound banks play back in response to voices and ambient noise, lights dim randomly, objects and rooms resonate against the drumming of small hammers. Through applying these systems of interaction and response the art object as a singular body disappears in order to reveal the broader, delicate interplay of multiple

bodies within social space.

Public

In two recent public projects, "Northpole Bridge" and "Connective Memory", this interplay is most pronounced. Constructed in the city Bochum, the "Northpole Bridge" project was designed as part of the construction and planning of the bridge in general, rather than being an artistic "add-on" to an already finished project. Wollscheid's work in essence consists of the design and construction of a lighting system. Responding to the movements of passers-by lights illuminate glass panels set inside railings along the bridge, and turn off as one passes. Creating a practical means of lighting public space the work in turn draws attention to one's own presence within that public space, how one both causes and receives effects, influences and is influenced by the architectural conditions which govern and aid one's movements. In essence, the lighting system exists as an "instrument" whose player is the public itself —— the individual body performs the work through chance interaction.

For Wollscheid, being an artist today means striving to overcome the object, to extend the object and its concerns into the social sphere, by utilizing the very inter-dependence of subject and object, this interaction of bodies within space. In this way, the role the artist plays is one of response —— to engage with the specifics of a situation, the spatial conditions, the social dynamics, the architectural tectonics, city planning, etc., etc. This ethos expands outward from the material object to engage with features of social reality —— here, reference points continually shift against public interference and the multitude, and are determined according to forces outside the artist's touch. "Northpole Bridge" in essence relies upon this interference —— it appeals to the unexpected throng of stimulation.

"Connective Memory", a second recent public project, further plays with this interaction and inter-dependence. Installed inside at a grade school in Trier, Germany, panels of audio sensing devices record sounds of students: laughter, conversations, the sounds of play, etc. Through computerized programming, the panels in turn play back these recordings when hearing similar sounds: laughter triggers laughter, banging triggers banging, voices trigger voices, etc. Through this interactive process one hears the sounds of one's own making, yet isolated and extracted. The processes at work in "Connective Memory" are spatial —— the work builds upon itself and reflects back the very forces (here, the sounds, articulations, vocalizations and noises of children at play) which constitute its density. Though "Connective Memory" also transforms this spatial density, its strata, by confusing the layers of meaning and their origin.

Exchanges
For Wollscheid nothing is hidden. The situation itself is the object. At work is a desire to remain within the uncertainty of social reality and the gentle instabilities of public space —— in essence, to remain susceptible to the viewer.
In considering the role of the artist Wollscheid also asks what is the role of the viewer. The question of audience for Wollscheid is tantamount to the making of work, to the structuring of systems of intervention. Through the dynamics of interaction, as a viewer one can not ignore the greater influences and effects of social reality, for Wollschied's work forces one to confront the very mechanics of this reality.

Wollscheid's installation work (as well as performance work) presents it system needing to be set in motion, awaiting the chance triggering. In decision making remains within the structural —— how to respond to
situation —— and what follows in essence is the work. Creating situations whereby the distance between object and viewer collapse, system and its place within social space converse, artist and audience switch places, one's sense of "privacy" is violated. There is an ethical demand in this, one which subtly incites awareness of the very role each is playing and allows access to the means of production (one begins to understand the light panels and their operation). This self-reflexivity undermines the pervasive alienation of the production and consumption dynamic, the hierarchical rules of art production itself, by making each viewer a participant with agency. Yet, this in turn causes anxiety, for as viewers we are asked to play an active role, to forfeit our enclosed interiority to the external

interplay of forces, to initiate the work itself. Yet we are already bound up within the work, a part of its production —— before we know it, the work is already in motion. As viewers we participate in a situation which asks from us more than we are used to: no comfortable distance between object and viewer, stage and audience, cause and effect.

Outside

Following this interest in social reality —— in essence, to remain "outside" —— Wollscheid's work does not veer into an autonomous zone, or lie snug within the confines of the gallery space: it resists phantasms of lyrical truth, even the comfortability of the contemporary art world, opting instead to confront the unexpected interference of social space, and the bureaucracies of city planning. In other words, Wollscheid stays within the "real". His work operates within the social, spaces in which life unfolds as an agitated flux, addressing the physical conditions of public space and public event. These conditions become positive constraints within which to produce work that in turn extend these very conditions.

In essence, his work functions as a call which we as viewers are always already responding to; in the flow of being one is already a part of relations, caught in structural conditions. The power of Wollscheid's work is that these conditions become a little more flexible, a little more

malleable, set in motion through a performativity which brings one's sense of self into a place of empowerment and self-reflection —— one is still susceptible to forces beyond one's control, yet how these determine experience is made apparent through a playful interaction.

About Face

In Duchamp's final work Etant Donnes, a situation is arranged whereby the viewer is asked to peer into two holes set in a wooden door. Through these holes one is presented with a uncertain scene, a tableaux depicting a nude woman prostrate beside a shimmering stream. One is unsure if she is living or dead, in pleasure or pain. She holds a gas lamp in one hand, offering illumination onto her own privacy, though she is only a body, her head escaping our view, just out of the scene. In this way, Duchamp obscures the face, and with it identity. He obscures one's ability to identify the body as a subject. Through this the moment becomes elongated, unresolved —— it is an uncertain spectacle.

The face, as Emmanuel Levinas theorizes, calls upon one as a subject to respond. As an ethical call, the face draws one into relation by a kind of pressure of responsibility: one can not not respond to the presence of the face, to the ethical call. In Etant Donnes Duchamp asks us to respond, to experience the unease of this ethical pressure by peering in, taking up our place just outside the door. Yet, in turn, this pressure becomes a device through which we not only witness the narrative scene, this strange tableau, but also the inner workings of art-making. The faceless art-object is an empty body which leaves us with our own gaze. The voyeuristic surveillance the viewer enacts in Etant Donnes brings into question the art / viewer relationship, the forces surrounding the art-object. The work forces one to consider how as viewers one is called upon to witness the art work, to play a role. Yet this witnessing is problematic, uneasy, for it never quite fulfills the demand.

An interesting effect over the course of years of viewers peering through the holes is the appearance of an impression that has been left on the doors themselves. This impression is one of a face –– with the two holes in the door standing in for eyes, the impression itself stares back at us as a face. It is there, an unmistakable identity, yet one which in turn is blank, a featureless face which stands for the multitude, for every face which has gazed through and all those which in turn will take up its place.

In essence, the work anticipates the viewer, it opens itself up to one's gaze, one's violating stare. Through this one can not help but feel self-conscious. This unease of the viewer is an ethical unease –– it forces one to consider one's own gaze as a violence, as a disruption, and visuality itself as an intruding force with real power. The face of the viewer penetrates the Duchampian door, yet what one is given, what one discovers in this penetration, is facelessness, leaving one to see nothing but one's own gaze, and to realize how as viewers we are participating in the work's very production.

The ethics of the face which Etant Donnes raises, Wollscheid extends to the whole body: the physical presence of the body and its gestures, from vocalizations, walking, blinking and laughing, listening, these become movements which reveal identity, marking the presence of the subject, through triggering effects –– the lights of the bridge, the clapping of performers, the playback of audio banks. Wollscheid's work

functions as the Duchampian door in that it anticipates the viewer, the unidentifiable passerby. In this anticipation art and viewer enter dialogue, public space and those who experience it converse, a conversation which may leave the artist behind, if only for a moment, yet which ultimately recuperates the art object not so much as an object but rather as a galvanizing presence activating the spaces and relations surrounding it.

When we consider a work of art in a physical sense, generally, it is distributed over a limited range of space-time when it is brought into its exhibition place. This means it is located in a specific space-time. Even if the work is multiplex, the work is located in each receptible space-time. We can regard this as an additional event/incident that is generated by movement in space-time. If the work is only a complete solid or a physical material, such that movement can be guided by the particle dynamics in the physical sense, then the work may exist as a self-reliant art object, and this art object will not depend on any place. At least, a self-reliant art object is expected to meet these requirements.

about an artwork operating on a specific place to let a potential activity emerge from it

minoru sato

On the other hand, an artistic production which depends on some specific place should be expected to somehow adress the issue of the potential activity in a specific range of space-time. Then we can certainly consider this activity to represent a proper disposition of the place, and the disposition can appear through various events which are generated by the activity. Thus this kind of art produces the place from some displacement within the place. It can bring out a proper disposition of the place through an additional event/incident generated by the displacement.

It can also create an image of a distribution of the place, such as an extension of the disposition in space-time.

As a range of space-time, the place is defined by a live space-time where the place's potential activity obtains an essential meaning for one's intervention, instead of a material space which is unrelated to one's intervention. A particular place such as this is familiarly found in the space in which we daily live. In this live space-time, one's own activities are always performed under the influence of the place. Therefore one's activity interacts with the proper disposition of the place. In a way, the proper disposition of the place can be characterized by the concerned persons within space-time. At the same time, one's activity (or our activities) suffers from some operation of the proper disposition. We can say that the disposition will be some physical, epistemological or organisational matter which concerns the various realms, and it is necessary that the disposition continues to operate on the space-time in order to support "place" itself. When we consider this relativity, we may find two directions of operation, i.e. from a person towards place and from place towards a person. On the other hand, we can consider that this has no specific direction. It seems possible to understand this as similar to the force between two magnets. This indicates a relativity that one side suffers from the other side's

operation, while the first side simultaneously suffers from the operation of the other. Essentially the word "interaction" in physics refers to this relativity. This word does not apply to the relationshsip presented by a chain reaction which has a specific direction of operation. Thus, we might be able to read this interaction into the potential activity of the place. In this regard, we can understand that an interactive work of art operates on the relativity between the place and the people who are involved with the place. In a way, the work of art becomes an in-between. It bears some displacement, as something from an additional event/incident which effects the relativity. This art product does not indicate an attraction which has a specific direction in oder to respond to a visitor –– a viewer or listener. It is necessary that the proper disposition of the place, which is found in the relativity as an interaction between the place and one concerned, emerges from the displacement through this work of art. To experience this art is to refer us to the relativity which is formed between the place and the visitor in this place. By this experience, we might become conscious of the proper disposition of the relativity, and also become conscious of the extension of the disposition in space-time. When I experience an interactive work created by Achim Wollscheid, I am led to think about the proper disposition of this kind of relativity. This thought relates to an experience which can be reflected in relativity with our daily space-time rather than something of a special experience. Furthermore it leads to multifarious concepts concerning a live place.

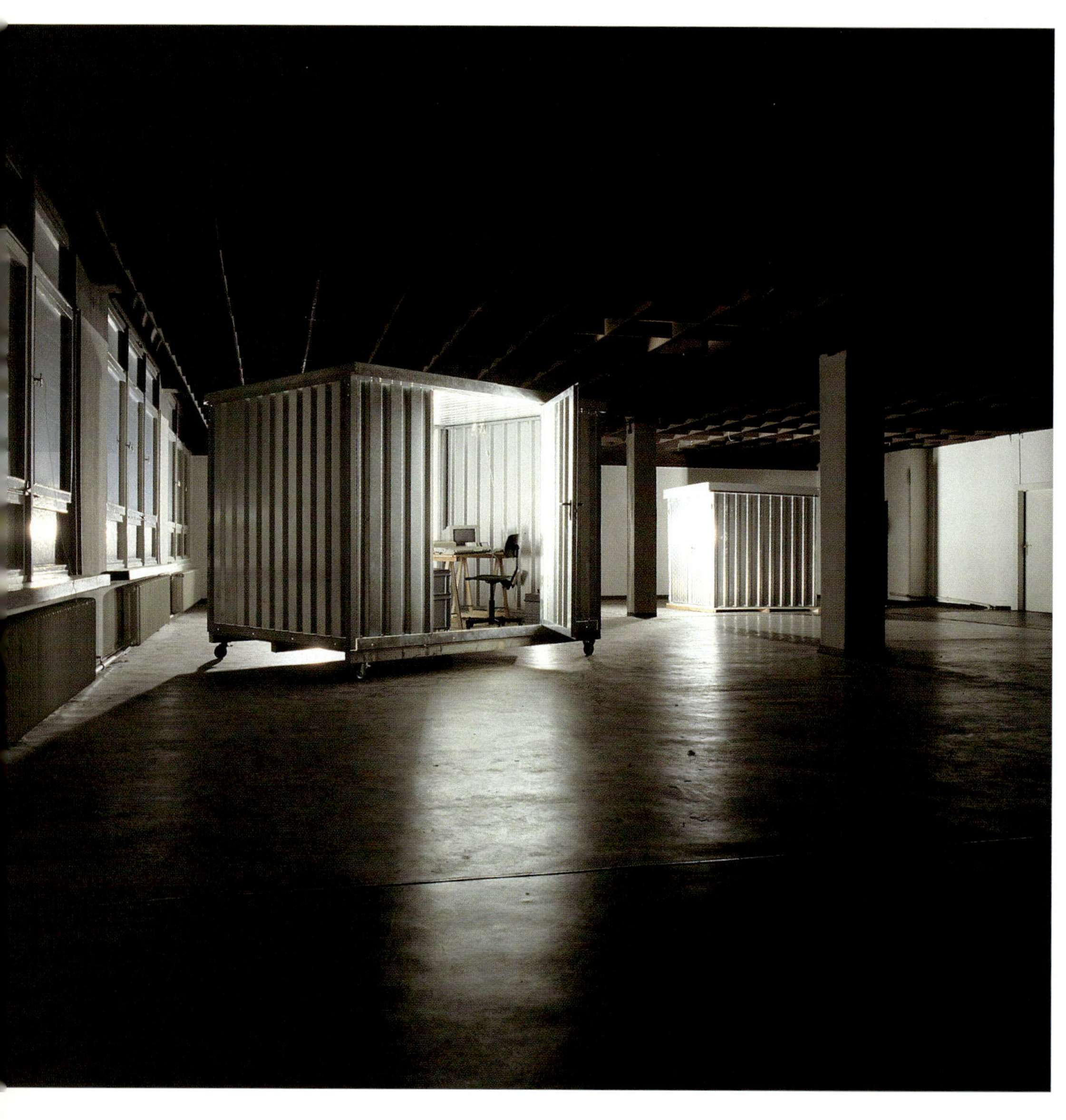

The size to which a sound generating body must expand in order to become a presence which projects a space with more than object-like, anthropocentric features was the question at hand when I attached a network of 1000 piezoceramic sound-transducers (small "loudspeakers" with a limited range) to a wall in the "Kunstverein Frankfurt". Driven by a sound generator, each speaker in the net constantly emitted the same sine wave at 1500 Hz. The extension and the permanence of the resulting sound-field created a multiplicity of "sound sources", because each of the listener's movements shifted positions in the interfering field of soundwaves and, therefore, altered the sound.

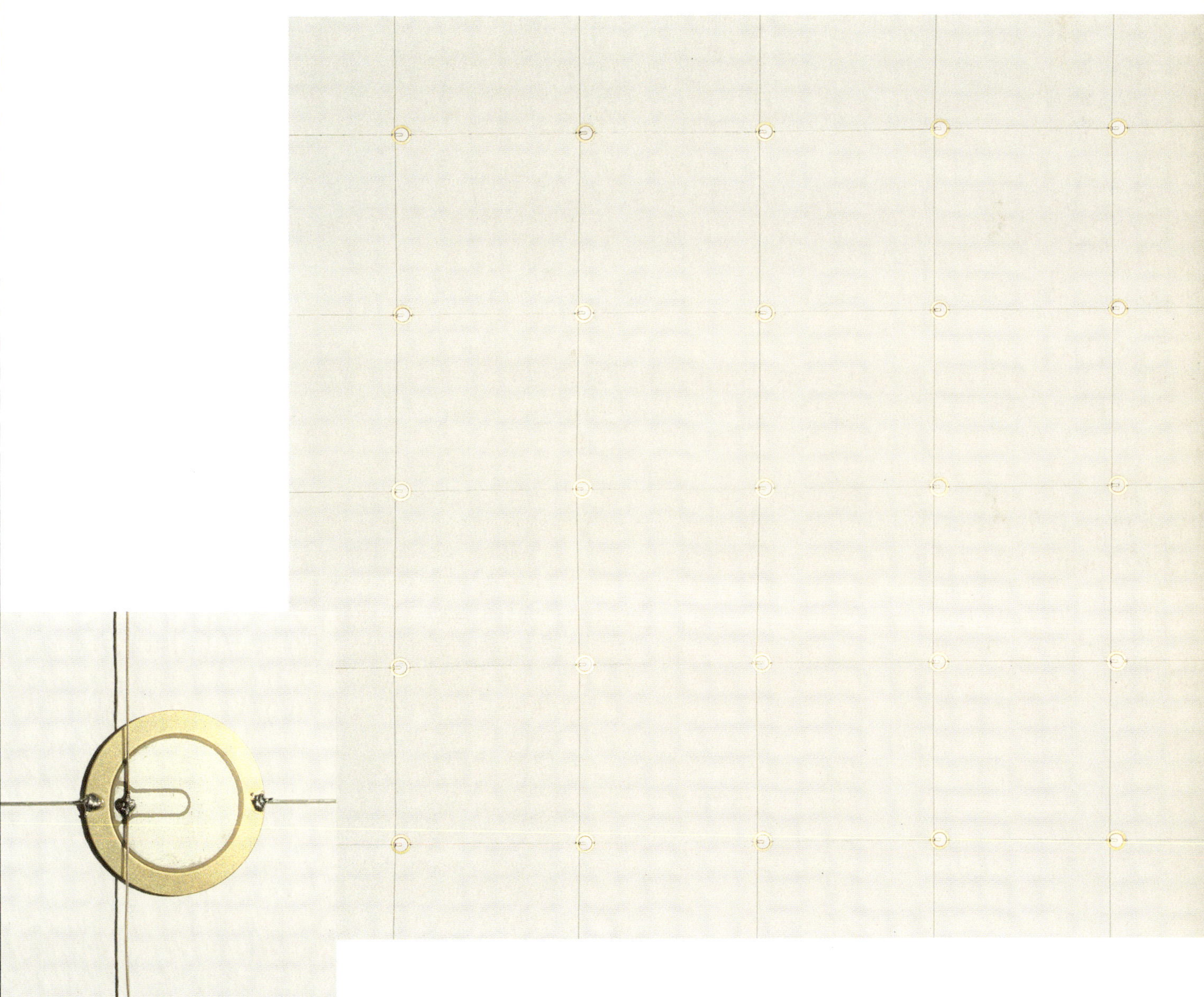

Wie groß ein klang-erzeugender Körper werden muß, um jenseits objekthafter, anthropozentrischer Form eine raumprojizierende Präsenz zu gewinnen, war Thema, als ich 1000 piezokeramische Klangwandler (kleine Lautsprecher mit begrenztem Frequenz-Umfang) an einer Wand des Kunstvereins Frankfurt an-brachte. Von einem Sinus-Ton-Generator gespeist, gab jeder Klangwandler dieselbe Frequenz von ca. 1500 HZ ab. Ausdehnung und Permanenz des resultierenden Klang-Raums schufen eine Vielzahl von "Klang-Quellen" – denn jede Positions-Änderung des Hörers/Betrachters im interferierenden Feld der Klang-Wellen verändert Klang-Wahrnehmung und Klang – bedingt durch das Doppler-Phänomen einerseits und der Erzeugung von Klangschatten andererseits.

This grid of 16 steel-plates was the installation that actually initiated the series of works in public space which included electronic sound generation. As with the following works in Trier (Basilika forecourt) and Frankfurt a.M. (ART Frankfurt), steel-plates cover piezoceramic sound-transducers, which –– receiving a sine-wave signal of about 1500 Hz from a sine-wave generator –– cause the plates to resonate. The steel-plates being assigned to a grid within the sidewalk mark a permanent, sonically and visually transgressable area in public space.

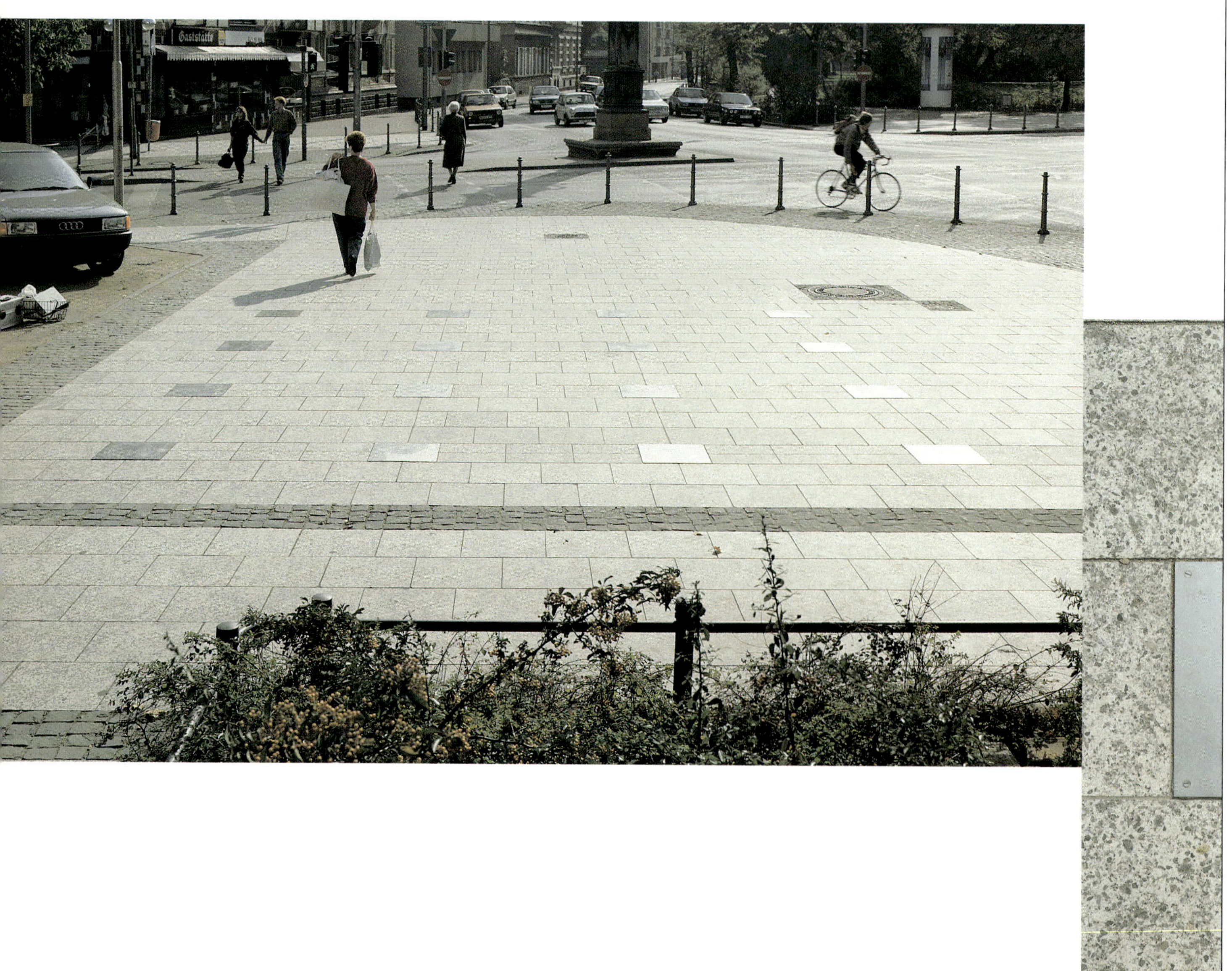

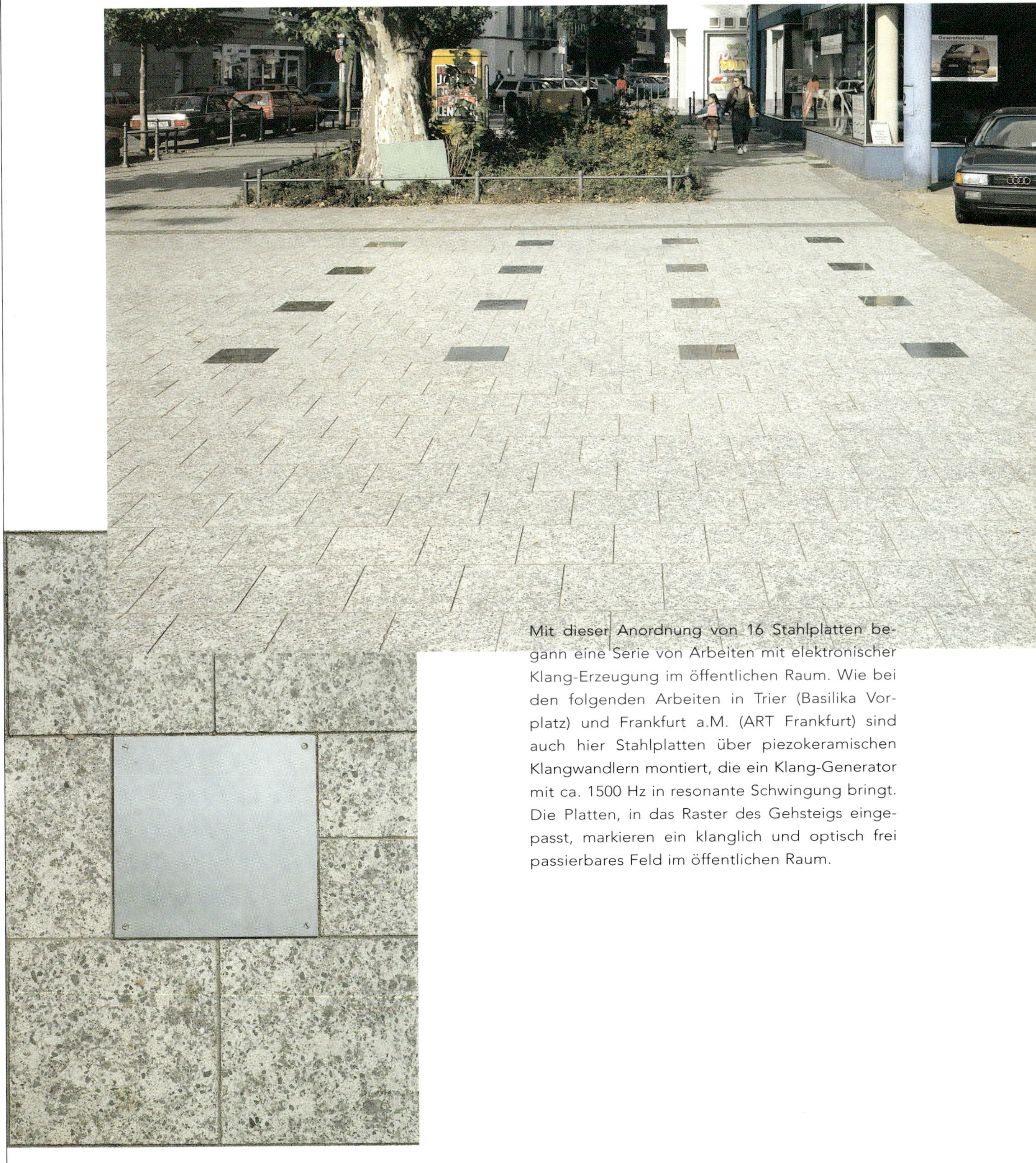

Mit dieser Anordnung von 16 Stahlplatten begann eine Serie von Arbeiten mit elektronischer Klang-Erzeugung im öffentlichen Raum. Wie bei den folgenden Arbeiten in Trier (Basilika Vorplatz) und Frankfurt a.M. (ART Frankfurt) sind auch hier Stahlplatten über piezokeramischen Klangwandlern montiert, die ein Klang-Generator mit ca. 1500 Hz in resonante Schwingung bringt. Die Platten, in das Raster des Gehsteigs eingepasst, markieren ein klanglich und optisch frei passierbares Feld im öffentlichen Raum.

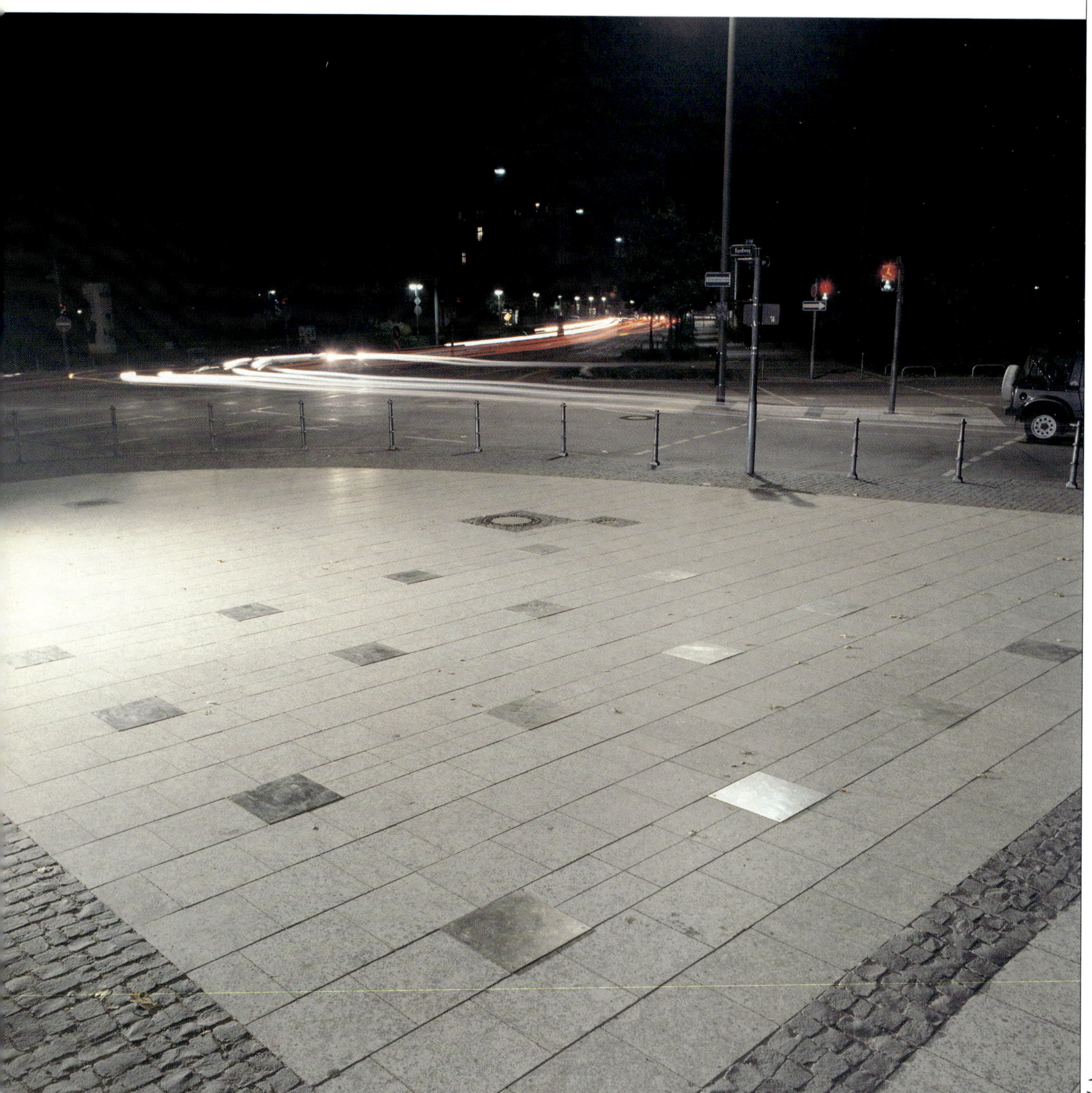

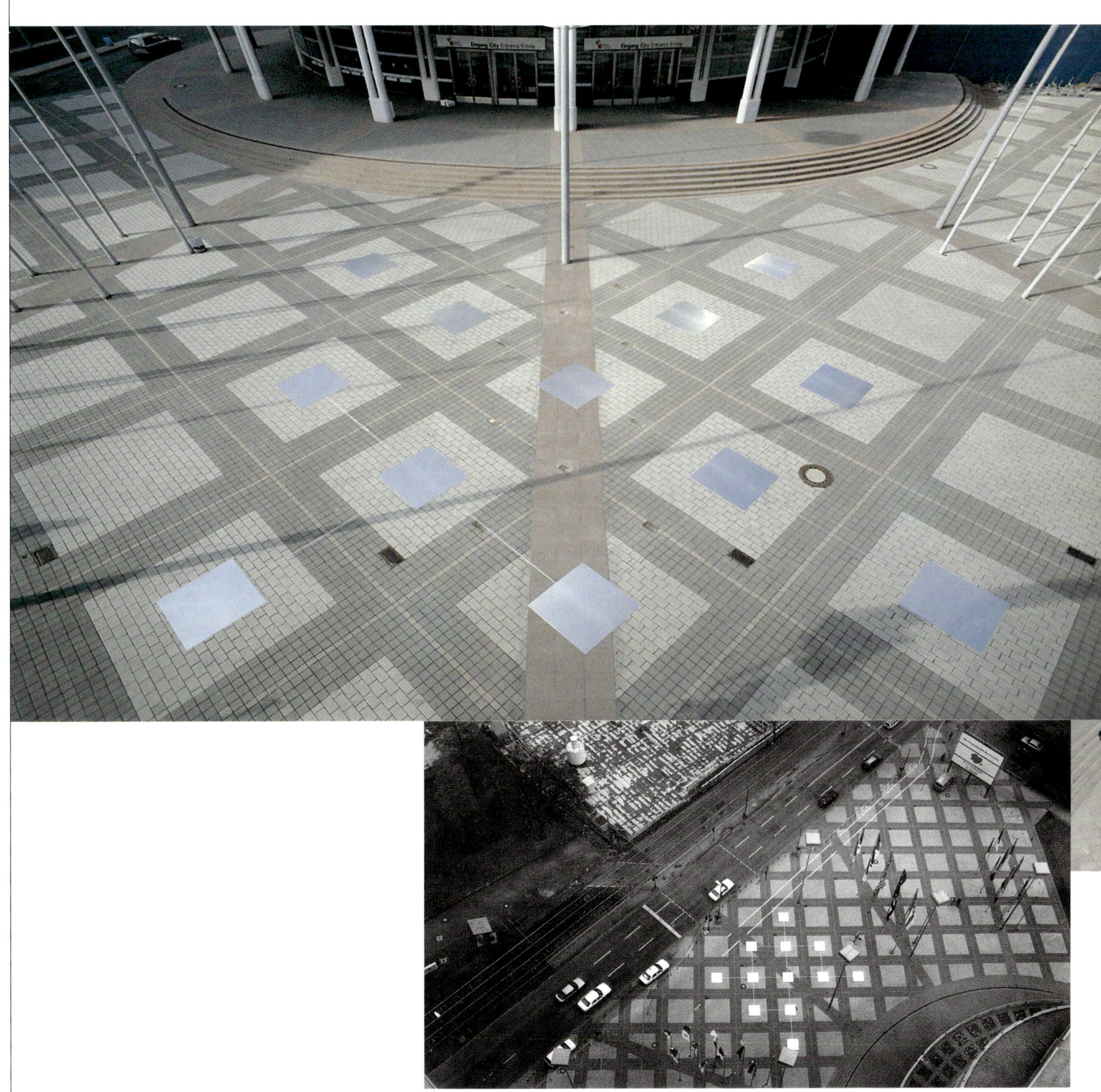

Eingang City Entrance Eingang
Eingang City Entrance Eingang

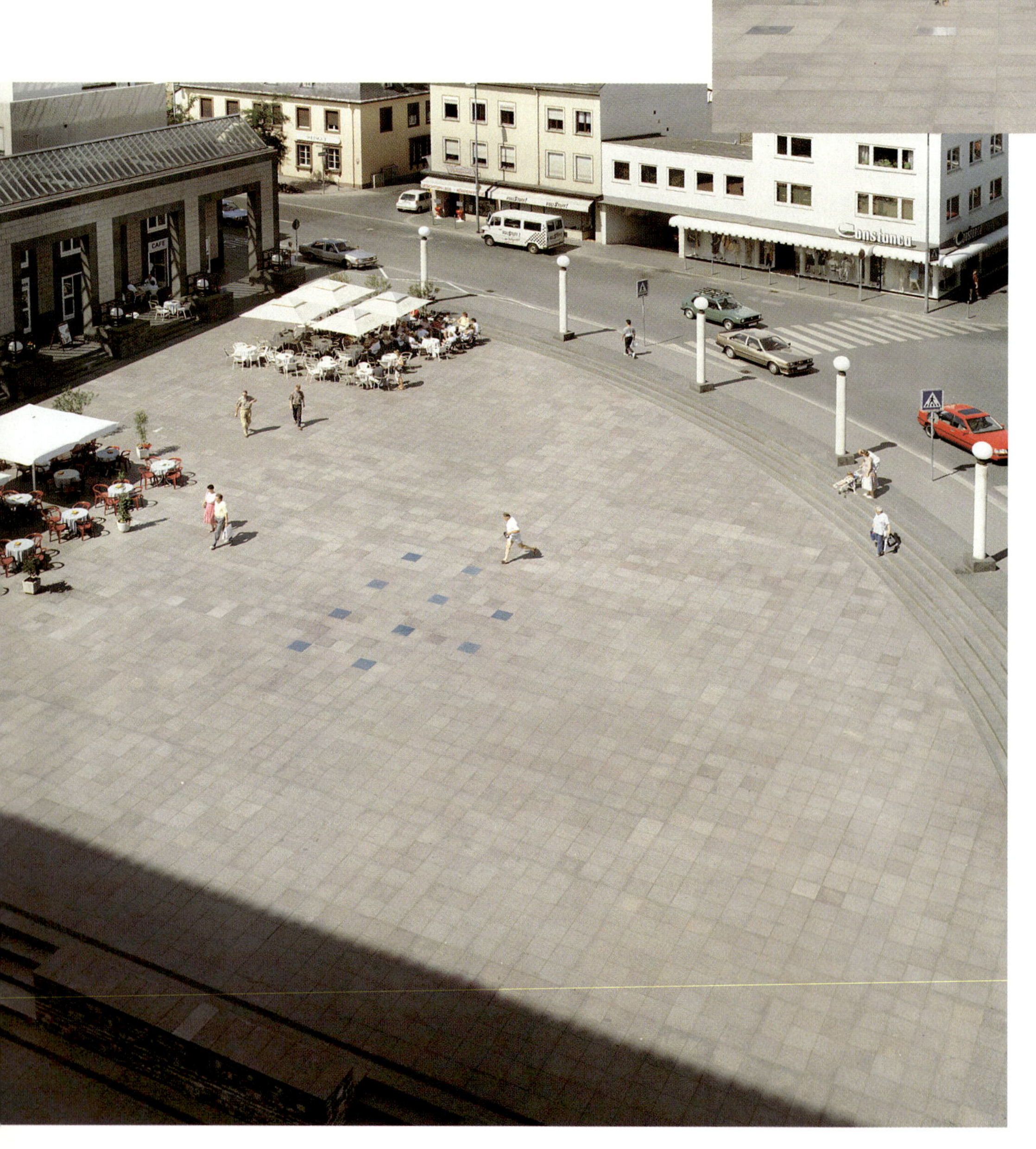

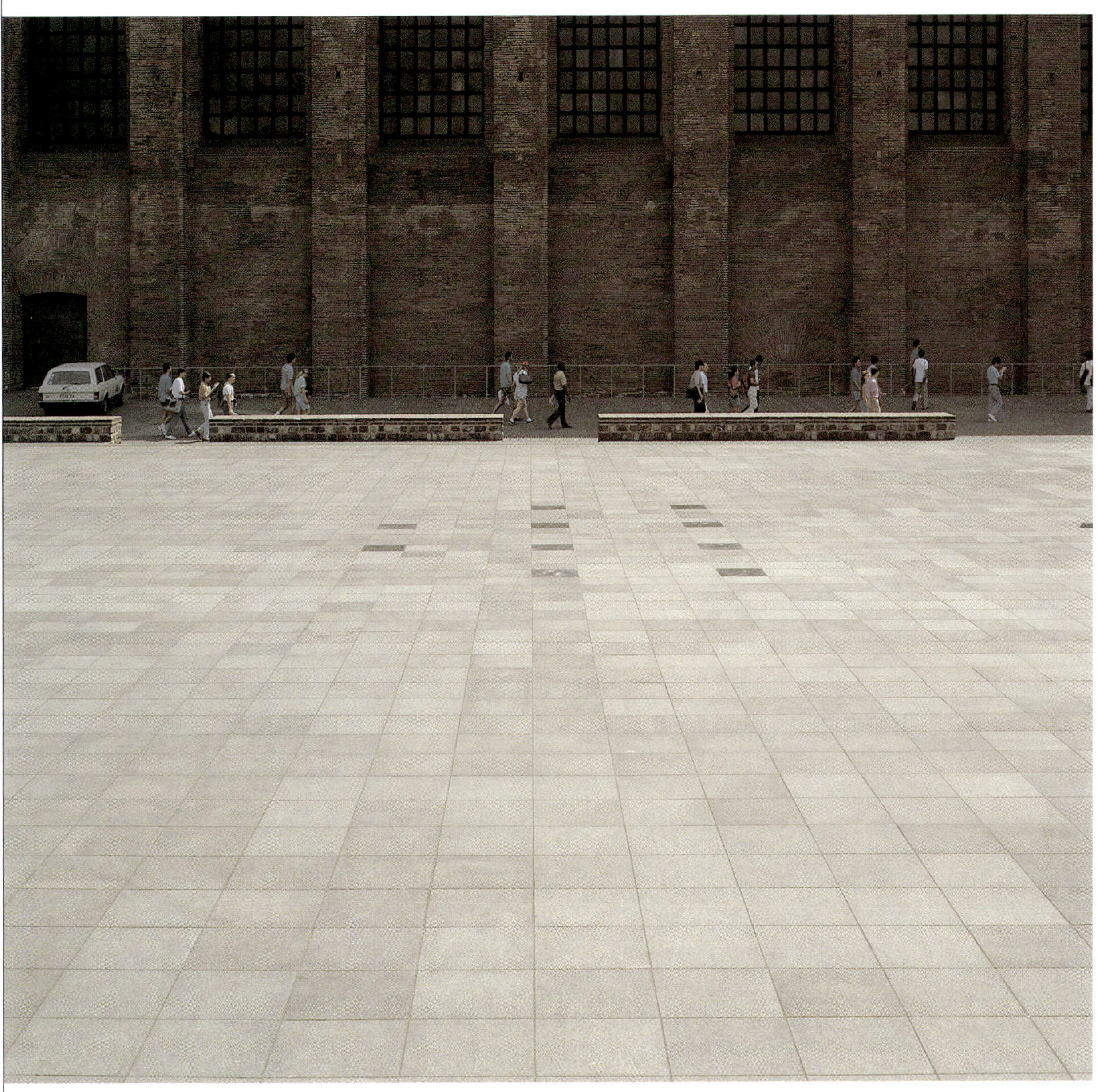

This bar, consisting of the defunct units of an escalator was assembled on the occasion of the dance-floor-event "sub and down" in a deserted Frankfurt subway. The light system, 16 strobe (flashing light) units, which backed the different acts these nights, translated sound samples into light movements.

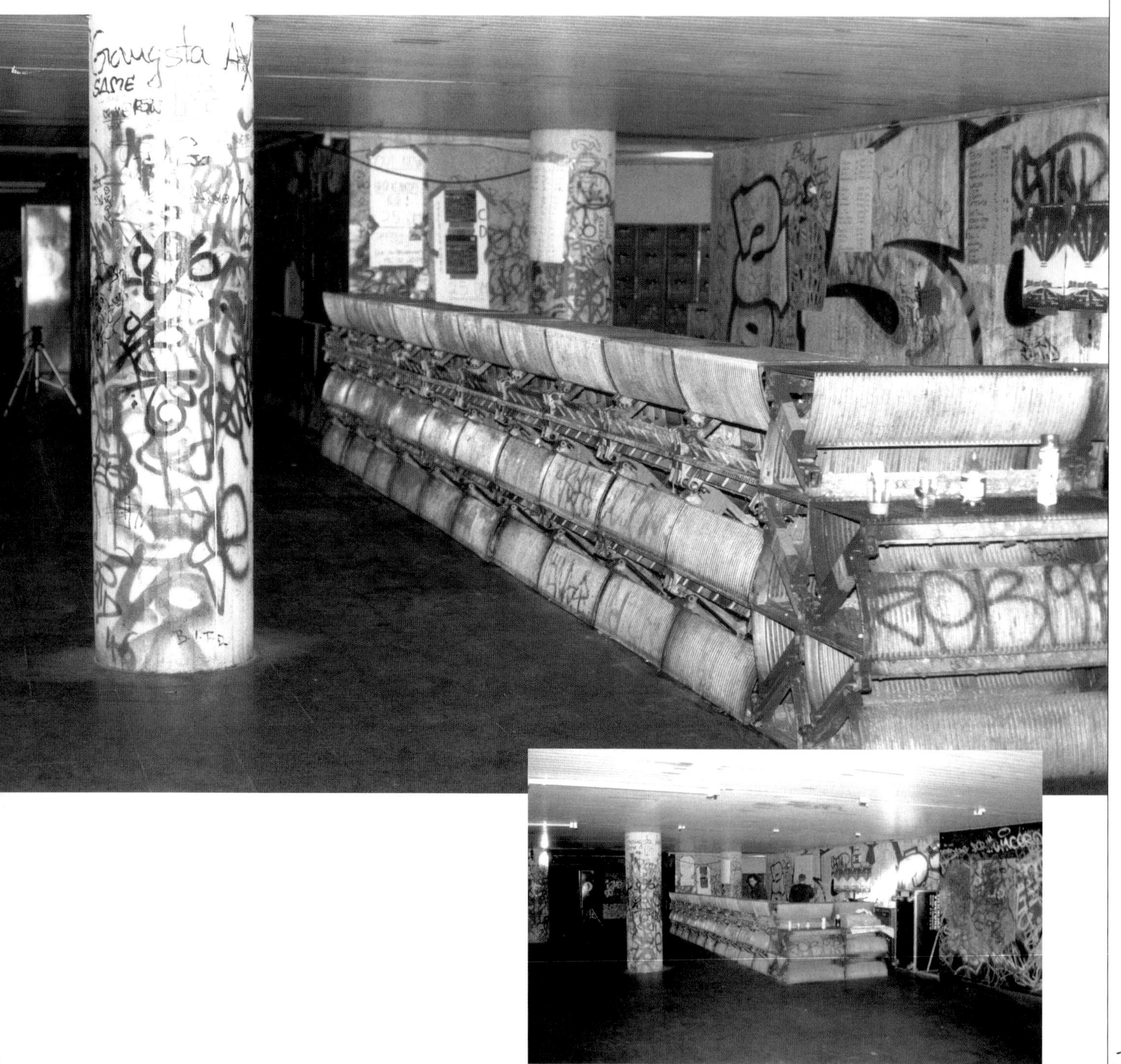

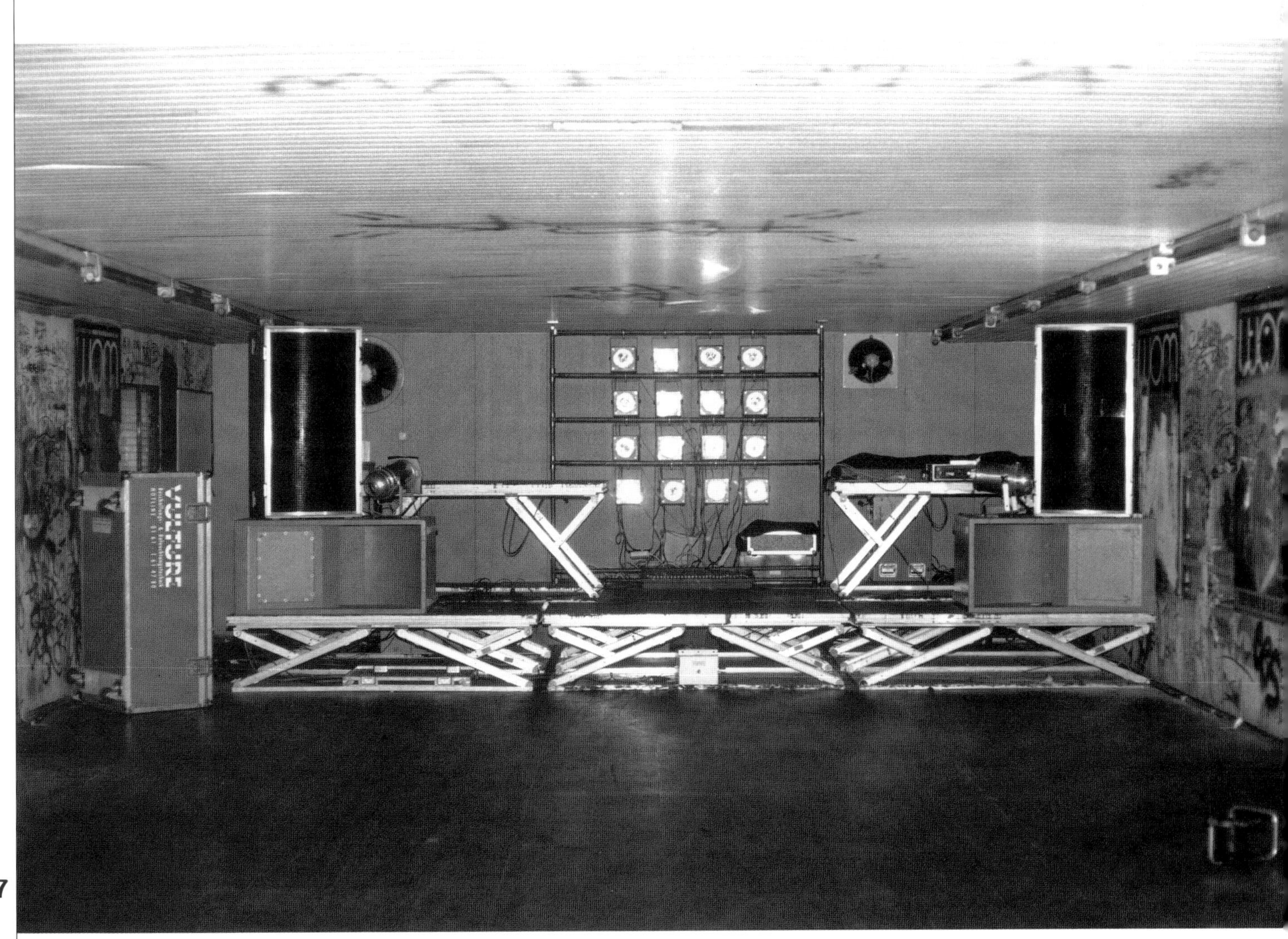

Diese Bar, entstanden aus am Ort gelagerten, ausrangierten Rolltreppen-Stufen, wurde anläßlich des dance-floor-events „sub and down" in einer Unterführung in Frankfurt gebaut. Das Licht-System, 16 Stroboskope, Hintergrund für die acts der beiden Nächte, übersetzte Klang-Samples in (Blitz-) Licht-Bewegung.

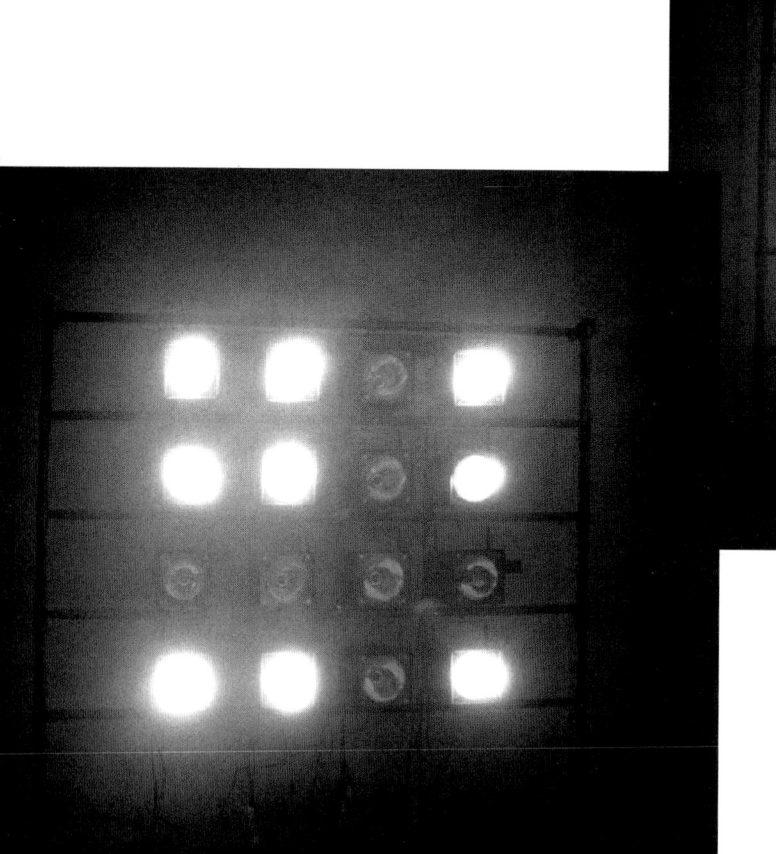

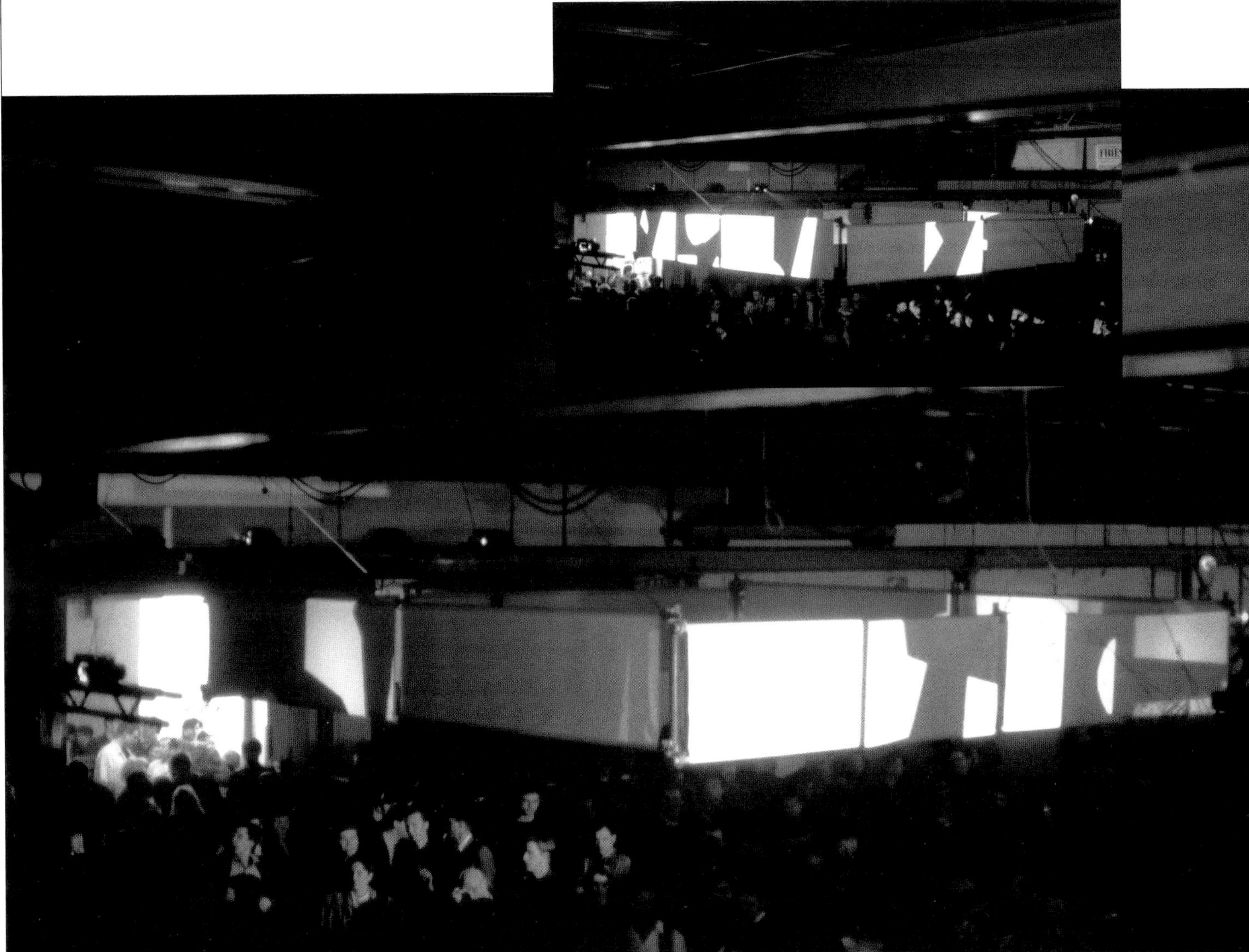

16 slide projectors, four facing each side of a rectangular projection screen, were suspended from the ceiling of a fair pavilion. All of the projectors were equipped with "mask" slides –– frames with varied geometrical cut-outs of black cardboard. When changing slides at maximum speed they produced a constantly warping light belt –– the light show for a dance event on 2 nights in 1992.

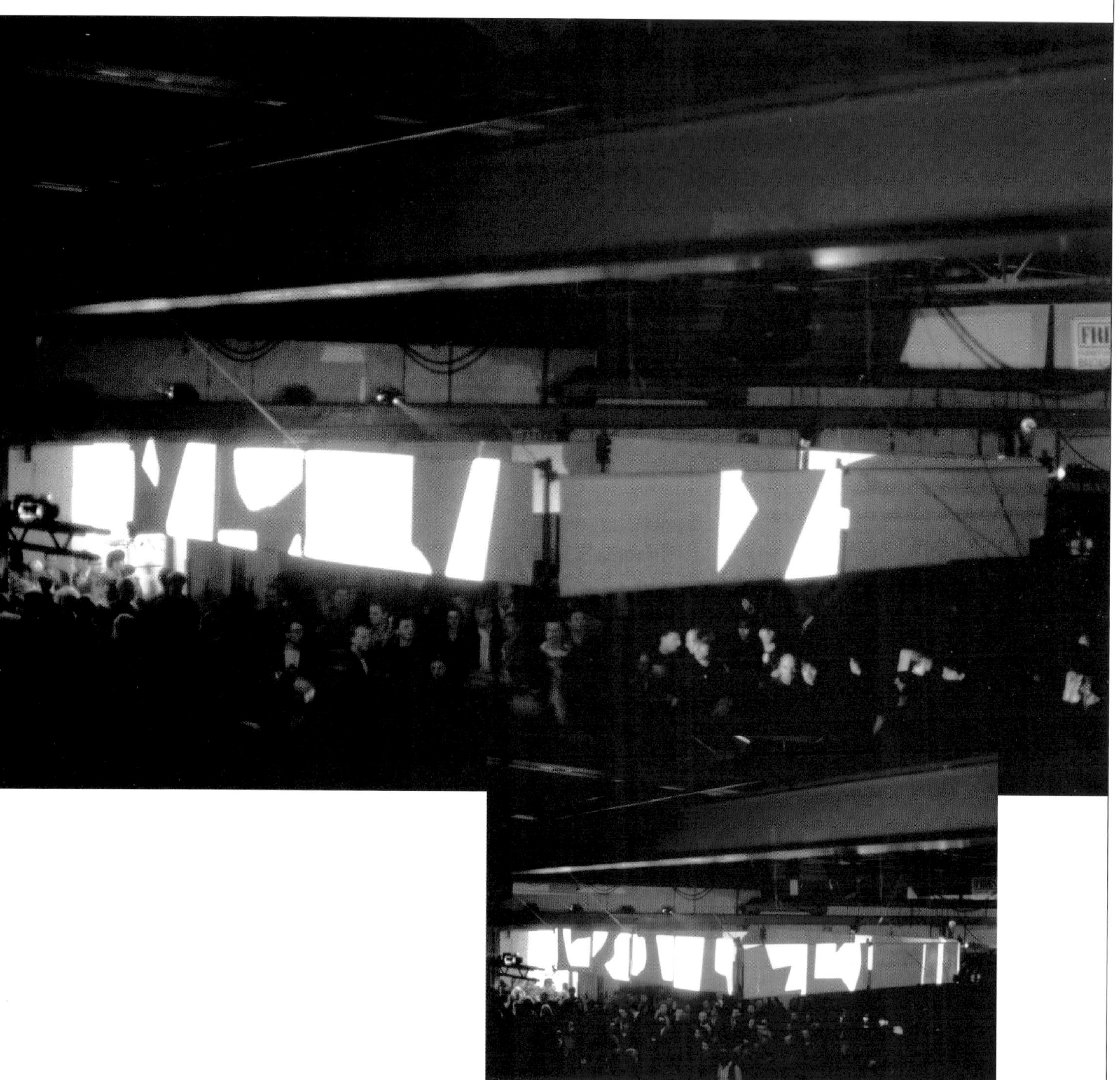

16 Dia-Projektoren, jeweils vier auf eine Seite eines quadratischen Projektions-Feldes strahlend, sind von der Decke einer Halle abgehängt. Alle Projektoren sind mit „Masken-Dias" bestückt, schwarzem Karton mit unterschiedlichen Ausstanzungen. Die einzelnen Dias mit maximaler Geschwindigkeit wechselnd, entwerfen die Projektoren einen sich ständig wandelnden Lichtgürtel – Licht für eine Tanzveranstaltung an zwei Nächten im Sommer 1992.

An installation for a festival. This event took place in a suburban "multi-function-hall" –– a space in which one would rather expect rock-concerts or dance-competitions than presentations of experimental music. The original plan was to borrow (rotating, mechanically driven) "Lesley" loudspeakers from local bands, to distribute them in the space and to emit sine wave sounds shifting in micro-levels. As it was impossible to locate or borrow such speakers the principle of the rotating system had to be recreated. Thus eight identical "stations" consisting of a tripod and two rotating loudspeaker systems (horn-drivers) were constructed. They were arranged in the hall in a regular pattern. During performance the rotating speakers emitted sine waves –– the resulting interferences and sound-layers led to a differentiated sound perception dependent on the position or movement of the listener.

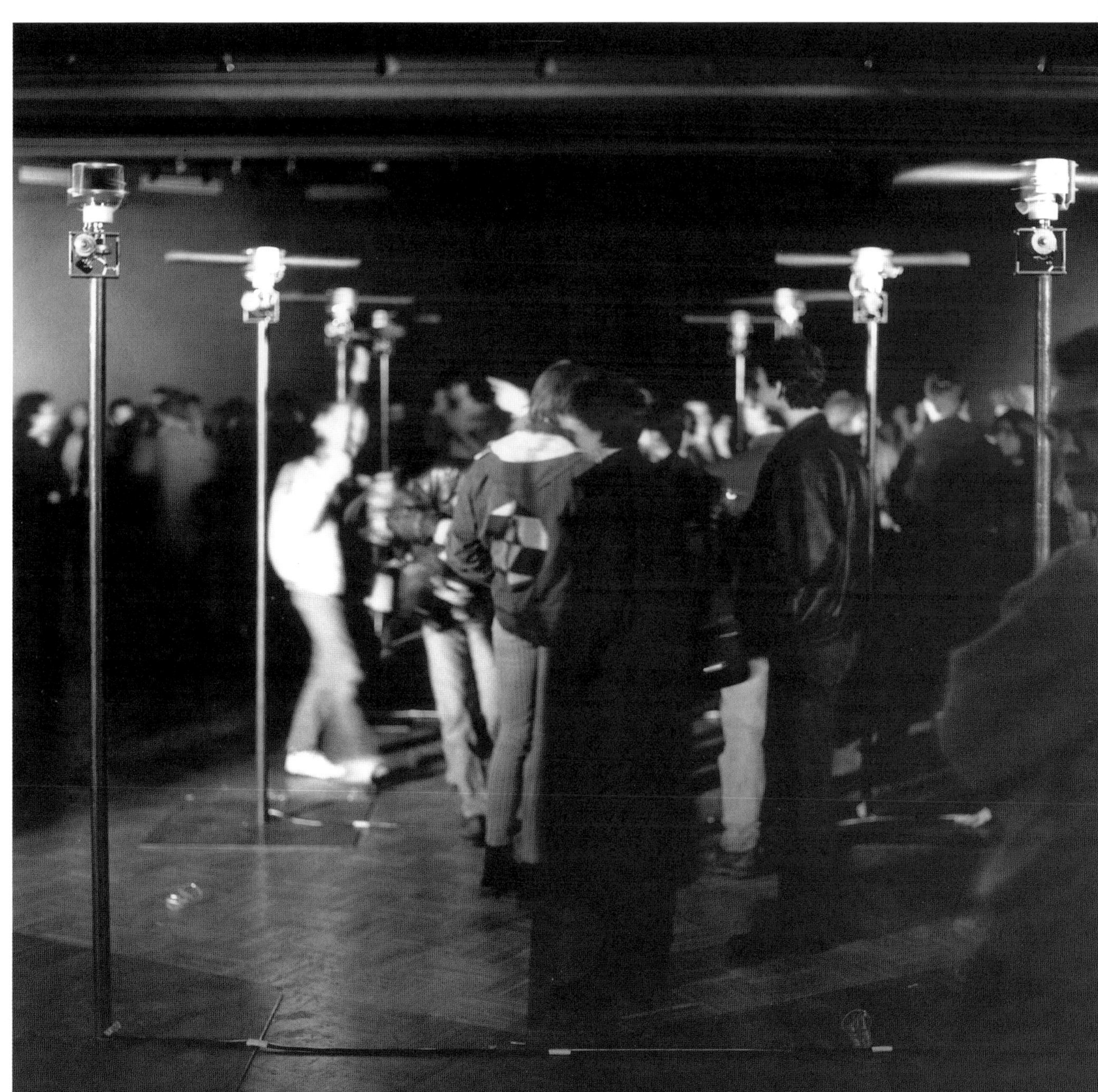

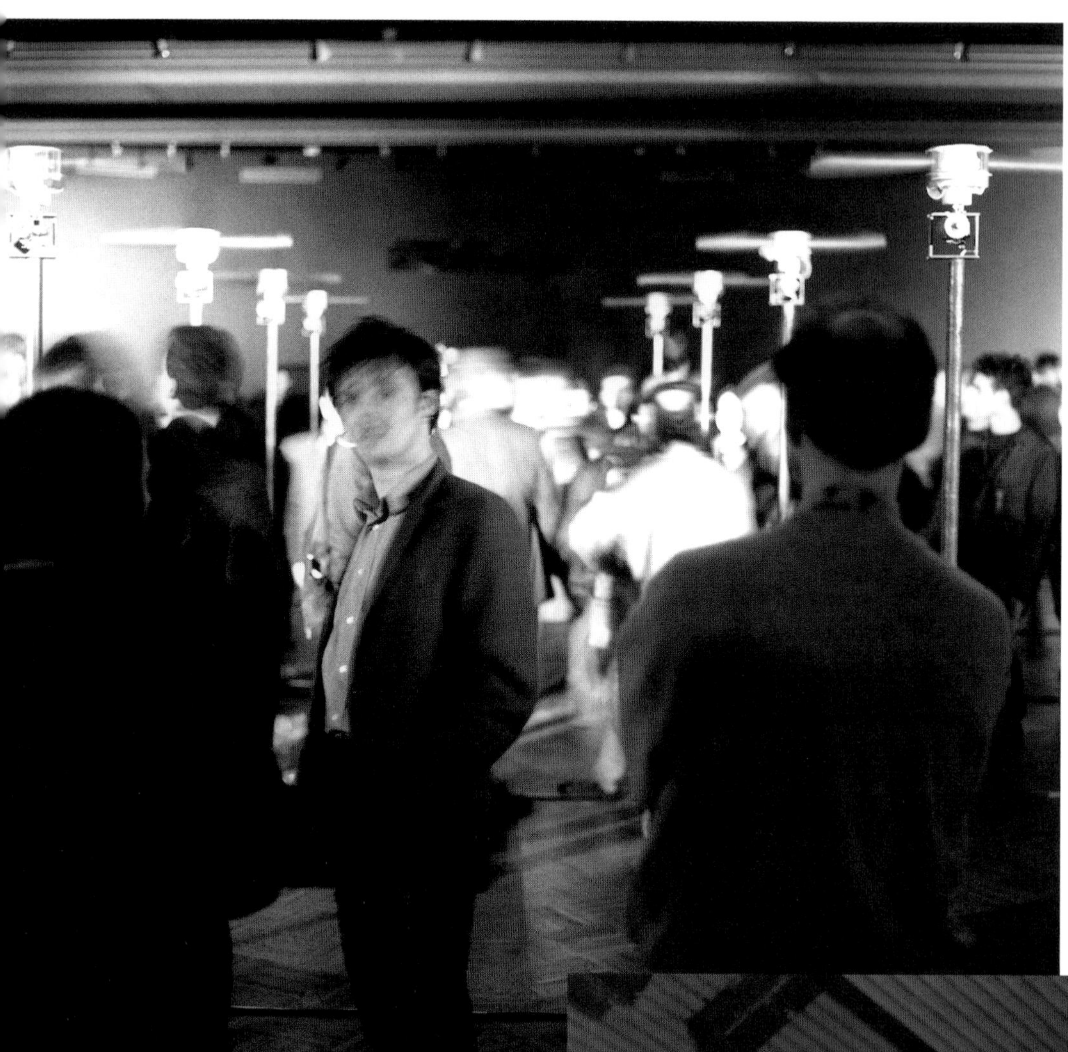

Eine Installation für ein Festival. Das Ereignis fand in einer Multifunktionshalle in der Banlieu von Nancy statt – ein Platz an dem man eher Rock-Konzerte oder Tanz-Veranstaltungen erwarten würde als ein Festival für experimentelle Musik. Ausgangsüberlegung war, (alte, mechanisch betriebene, rotierende) „Lesley" Lautsprecher von ortsansässigen Bands zu leihen, sie in der Halle zu verteilen und darüber sich in Mikrotonintervallen verschiebende Sinus-Töne abzuspielen. Da es sich als unmöglich erwies, solche Lautsprecher zu leihen, wurde das Prinzip des rotierenden Systems nachgebaut: Acht identische „Stationen", bestehend aus einem Stativ und zwei drehbar gelagerten Horn-Treibern. In der Halle wurden sie in einem regelmäßigem Muster aufgestellt: in möglichst gleicher Entfernung voneinander und von der Wand. Während der „Vorstellung" ergaben die ausgestrahlten Sinus-Töne ein differenziertes Klangbild – jeweils sich verändernd mit der Position und Bewegungsgeschwindigkeit des einzelnen Hörers.

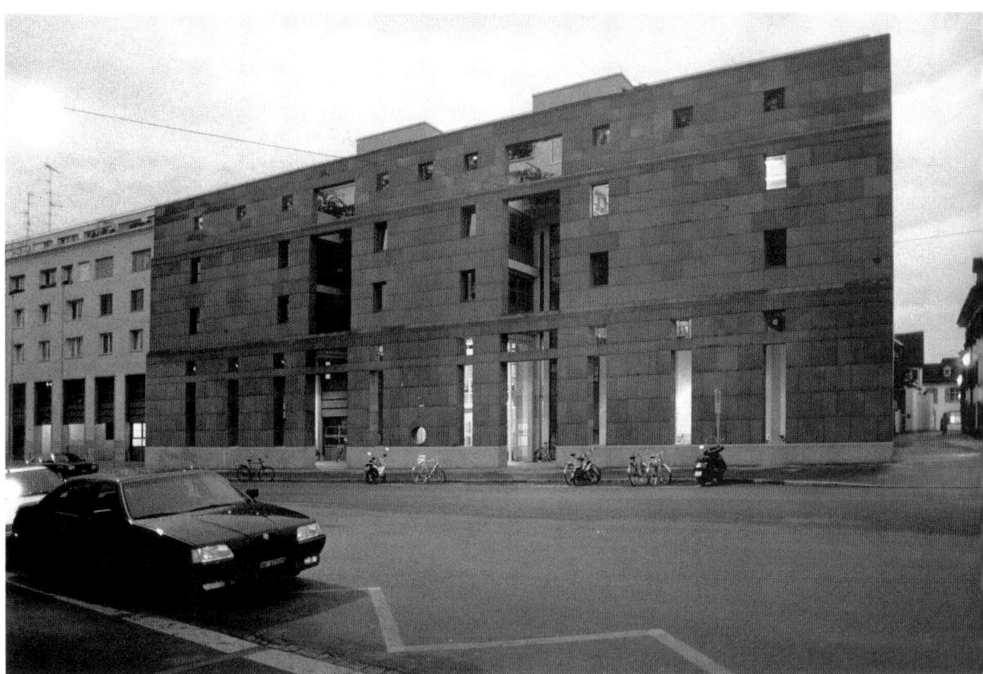

This system consisted of 16 flashing lights, which simultaneously flashed in shifting time intervals. The time shifts (varying between 30 and 90 seconds) were determined by (hardware) chance operation. As the building obviously quotes the medieval city-wall, the flashes were positioned in its embrasures to draw attention to a happening that is gone, the moment one has noticed it.

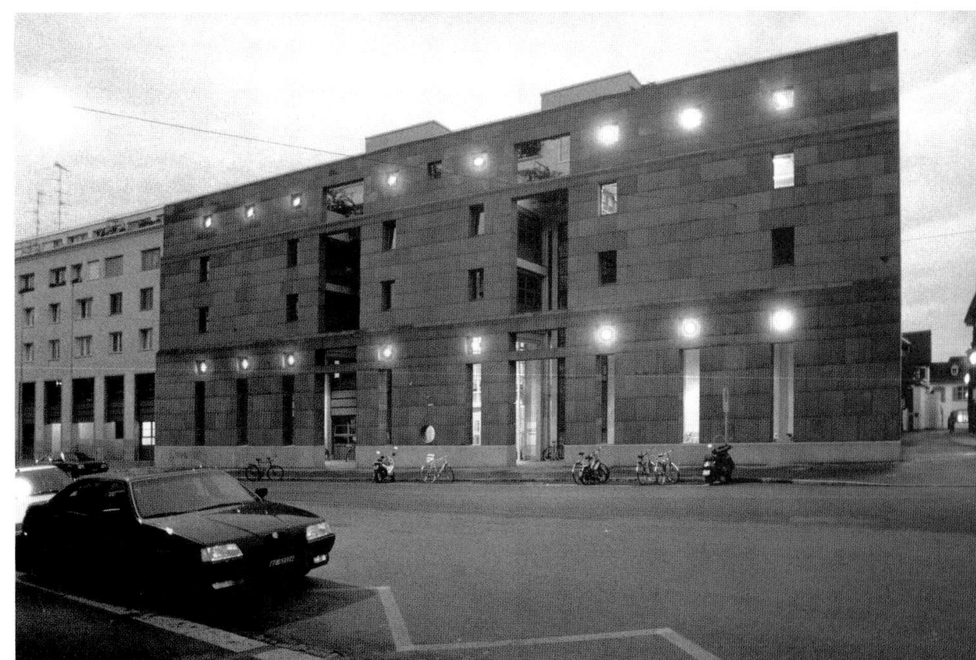

Dieses System bestand aus 16 Stroboskopen, die jeweils gleichzeitig, doch in wechselnden Zeitabständen kurz aufblitzten. Die Zeitverschiebungen (zwischen 30 und 90 Sekunden) wurden von einem Zufallsgenerator gesteuert. Da das Gebäude offensichtlich eine mittelalterliche Stadtmauer zitiert, wurden die Blitze in den Schießscharten positioniert – um die Aufmerksamkeit auf ein Ereignis zu lenken, das vergangen ist, wenn man es wahrnimmt.

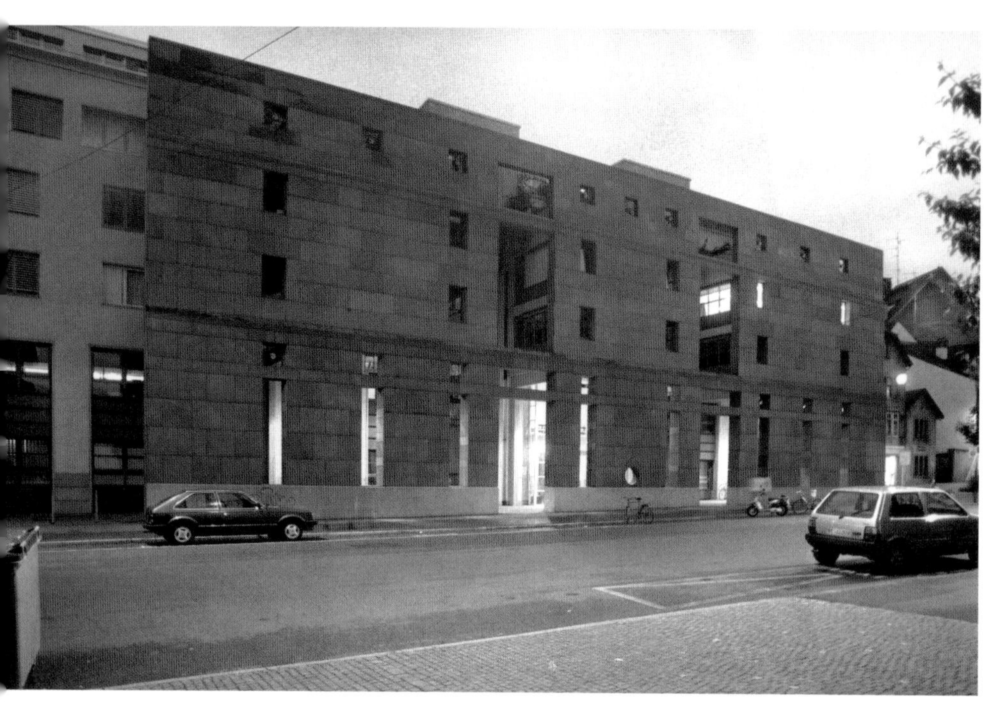

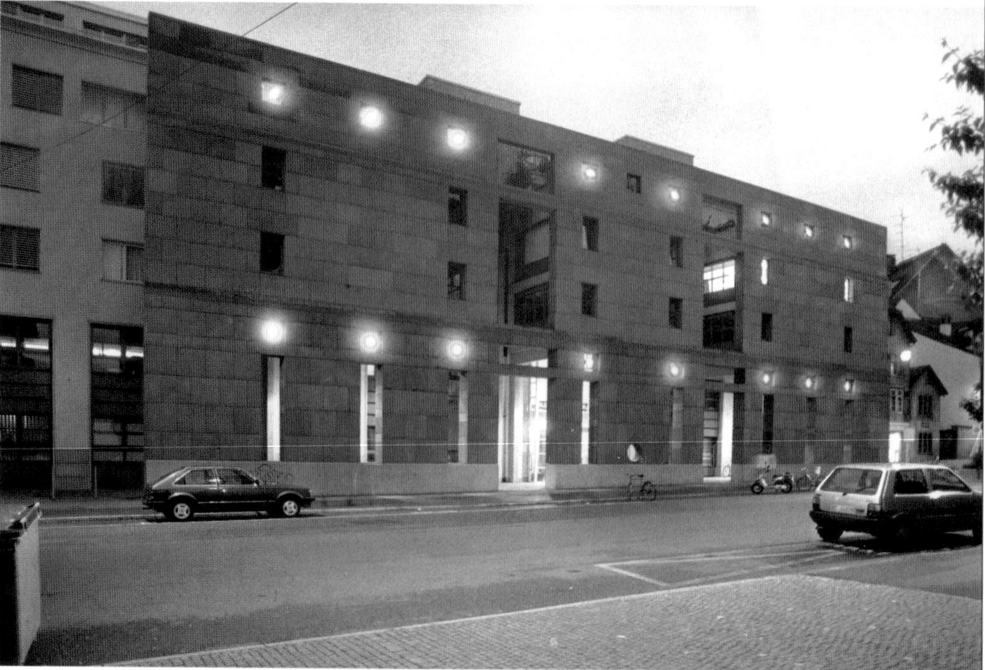

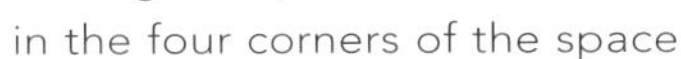

A collaboration between Joachim Pense, Stefan E. Schmidt, Roger Schönauer, Charly Steiger, Ralf Wehowsky and Achim Wollscheid. SLP combined a sound installation, a computer generated sound-recycling and a composition. It transferred the achievements of collaborative work and SELEKTION's development of tape music to the realm of live-presentation. Four operators standing on a pedestal in the middle of the audience play different passages of NNNN! (DLP, SELEKTION 1986) from a turntable as directed by an electronic score. The sonic information produced passes through an interface: depending on computer-directed composition the eight respective channels can be switched "on" or "off" and directed to the loudspeakers in the four corners of the space.

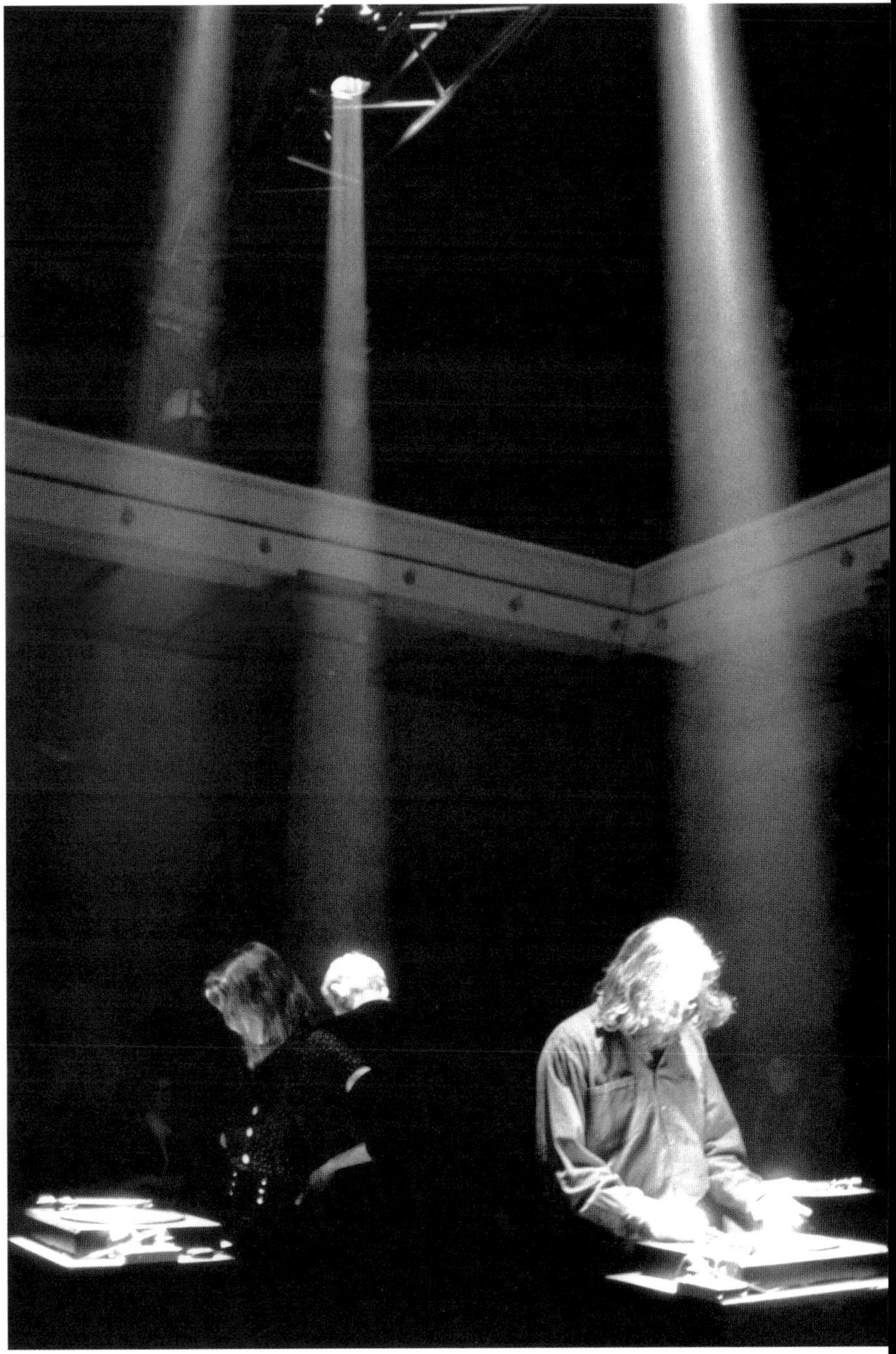

Eine Zusammenarbeit von Joachim Pense, Stefan E. Schmidt, Roger Schönauer, Charly Steiger, Ralf Wehowsky und Achim Wollscheid.
SLP umfaßte eine Klang-Installation, ein computergenereriertes sound-recycling und eine Komposition. Das Projekt versetzte dabei die Ergebnisse verschiedener Kollaborationen und der tonbandmusikalischen Entwicklungen innerhalb von SELEKTION in den Bereich der Live-Präsentation. Vier Operateure stehen auf einem podestartigen Element inmitten des Publikums und spielen verschiedene Passagen der LP NNNN (SELEKTION 1986) – dabei geleitet von einer elektronischen Notation. Die so erzeugte Klanginformation (acht Kanäle) wird einem Schalt-element zugeführt, wo sie, gemäß einer computergesteuerten Kompositions-Matrix gelöscht oder durchgelassen wird und entsprechend auf einem oder mehreren der vier in den Raum-ecken befindlichen Lautsprechern erklingt.

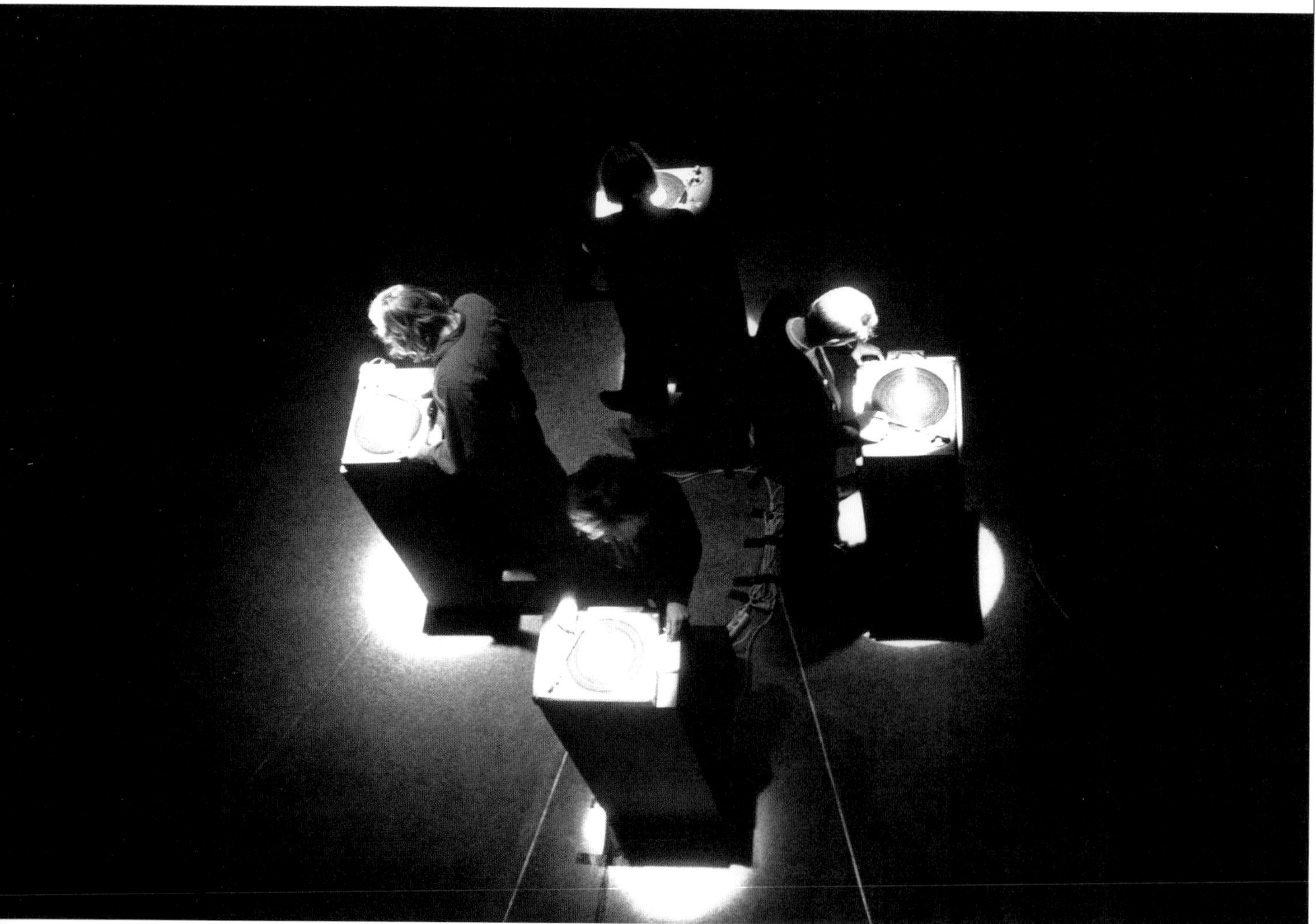

A certain unease with the atmosphere of the corridor-system in the newly built Frankfurt tax office led to an implementation of artistic works using light, that would somehow interrupt or change the present uniformity. As this building is a fully computerized, the nostalgic notion of such tax office corridors hosting a permanent traffic of people and files cannot be maintained. To paraphrase the question of who actually moves (and for what purpose), I decided to let the light move. All extant corridor lamps in two floors are therefore equipped with an additional small operator. The primary "on/off"-function of the lamps is now superimposed by a secondary function: an individual "dimming" of each lamp, a soft but noticeable shift of light intensity in about 200 intervals per day. Each operator consists of an individual memory and a trigger system directed by a co-ordinated time code. The program thus transforms the state of a unit according to a (composed) time pattern. The resulting changes of light interact in groups, form individual movements or highlight certain corridor-segments for a short time.

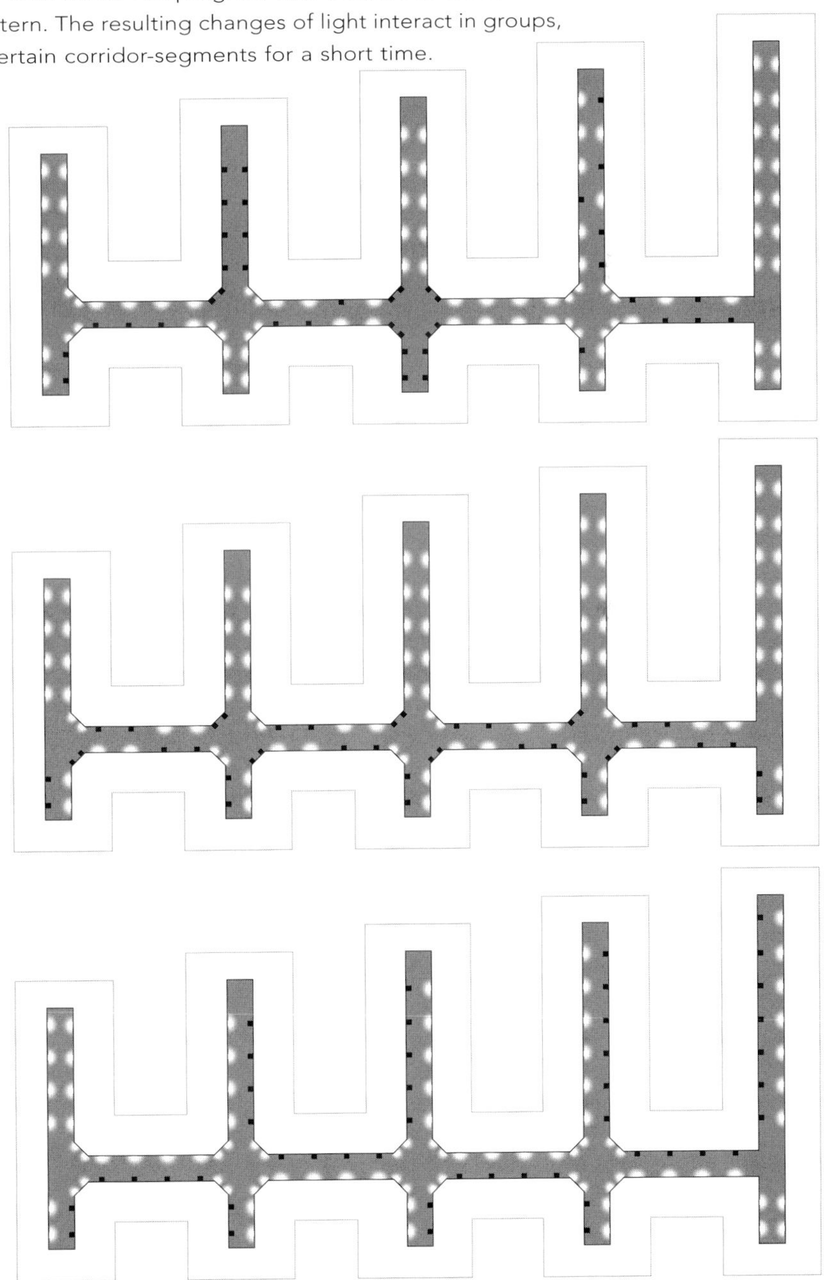

Ein gewisses Unwohlsein mit der Atmosphäre in den Gängen des neu entstandenen Frankfurter Finanzamts führte zu einer zusätzlichen Implementierung von Lichtkunst – die die bestehende Uniformität der Gänge verändern oder unterbrechen sollte. Da dieses neue Gebäude ein voll computerisiertes ist, kann die nostalgische Vorstellung von Finanzamtskorridoren als Verkehrsadern für die Bewegung von Menschen und Akten(wagen) nicht aufrechterhalten werden. Um die Frage, wer sich (zu welchem Zweck) bewegt, zu paraphrasieren, bewegt sich das Licht. Alle bereits vorhandenen Flurlampen sind mit einem Schaltelement nachgerüstet: die zugrundeliegende „Ein /Aus"-Funktion wird um eine weitere ergänzt: einer individuellen Dimmung jeder einzelnen Lampe, einer leichten, aber wahrnehmbaren Veränderung der Licht-Intensität in ungefähr 200 Schaltvorgängen pro Lampe und Tag. Jedes Schaltelement besteht aus einem Speicher (mit dem jeweils individuellen Programm für jede Lampe) und einem Trigger, der von einer Schaltuhr gesteuert ist. Das Programm verändert nun den Zustand der jeweiligen Einheit in bezug auf ein (komponiertes) Zeitraster. Die resultierenden Licht-Veränderungen lassen Gruppen von Lampen interagieren, formen individuelle Bewegungen, oder betonen bestimmte Korridor-Segmente für kurze Zeit.

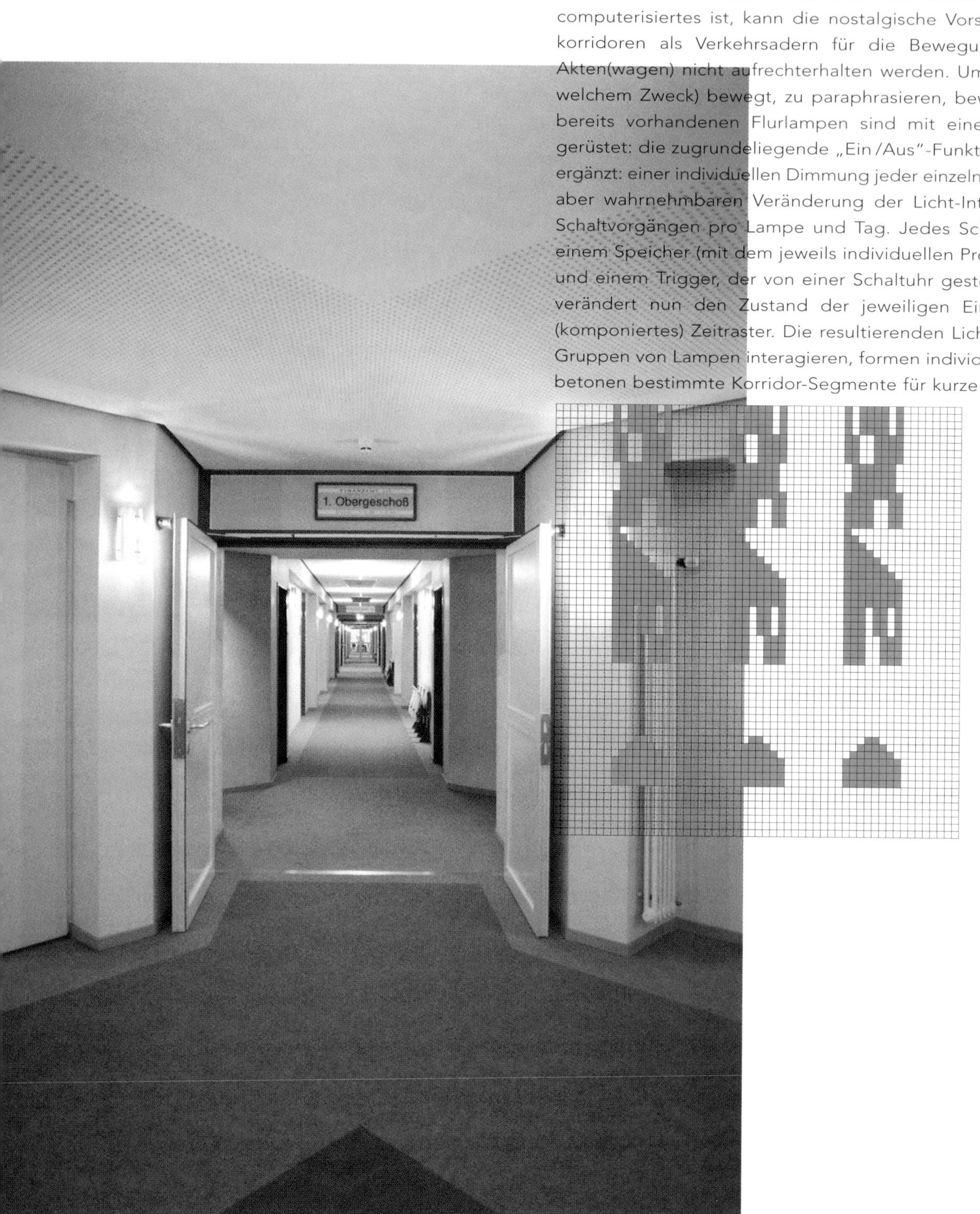

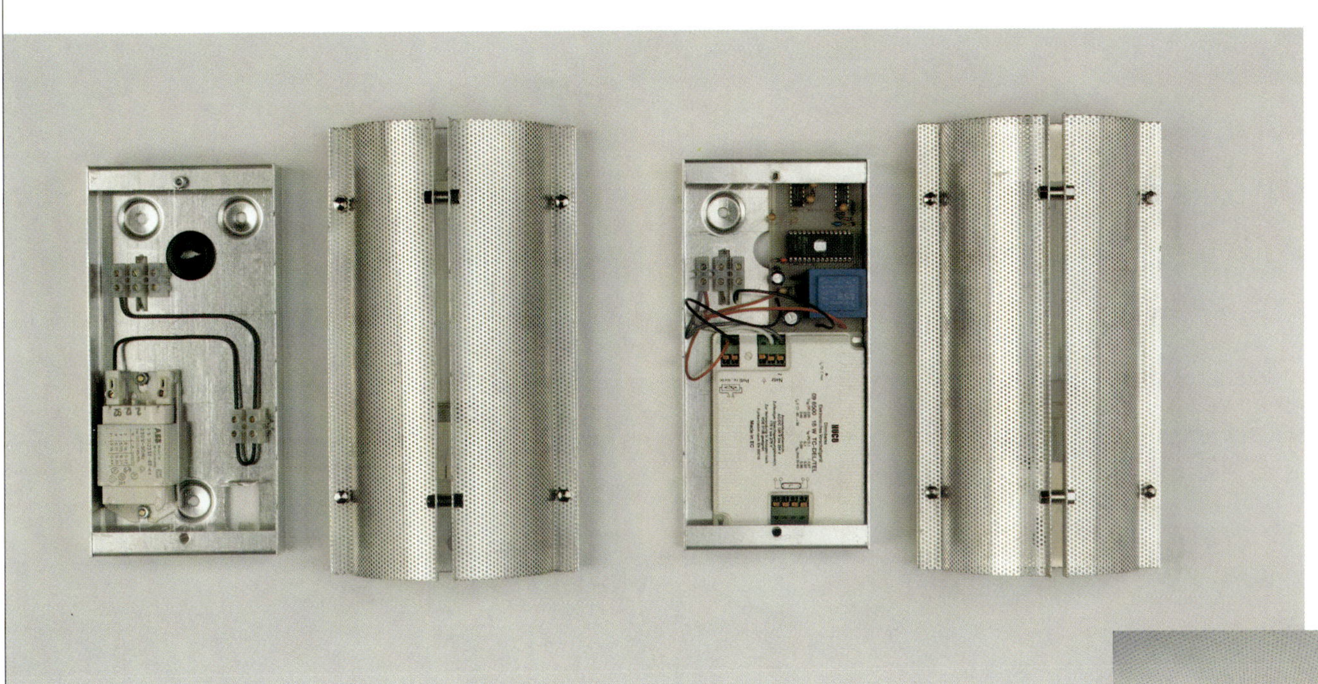

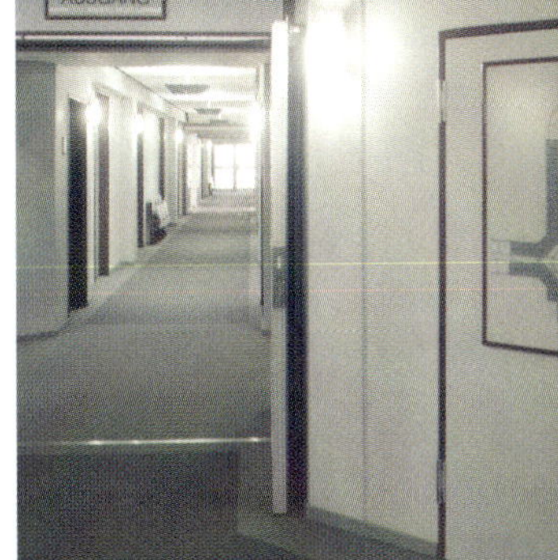
AUSGANG

A light system built for a friend of mine, who commissioned a lamp. As the balcony of the flat is designed to be the outdoor continuation of the inside, the idea was to "switch on the balcony". The technical set-up consists of eight focused lamps on both ends of the balcony. The light beams of the lamps form a "zebra"-stripe carpet which is in permanent motion. Each of the 16 lamps is independently connected to a dimmer system that defines length, speed and intensity for the single dimming process of each lamp. The dimming system is computer-generated and connected to a randomizer which guarantees the uniqueness of each single pattern.

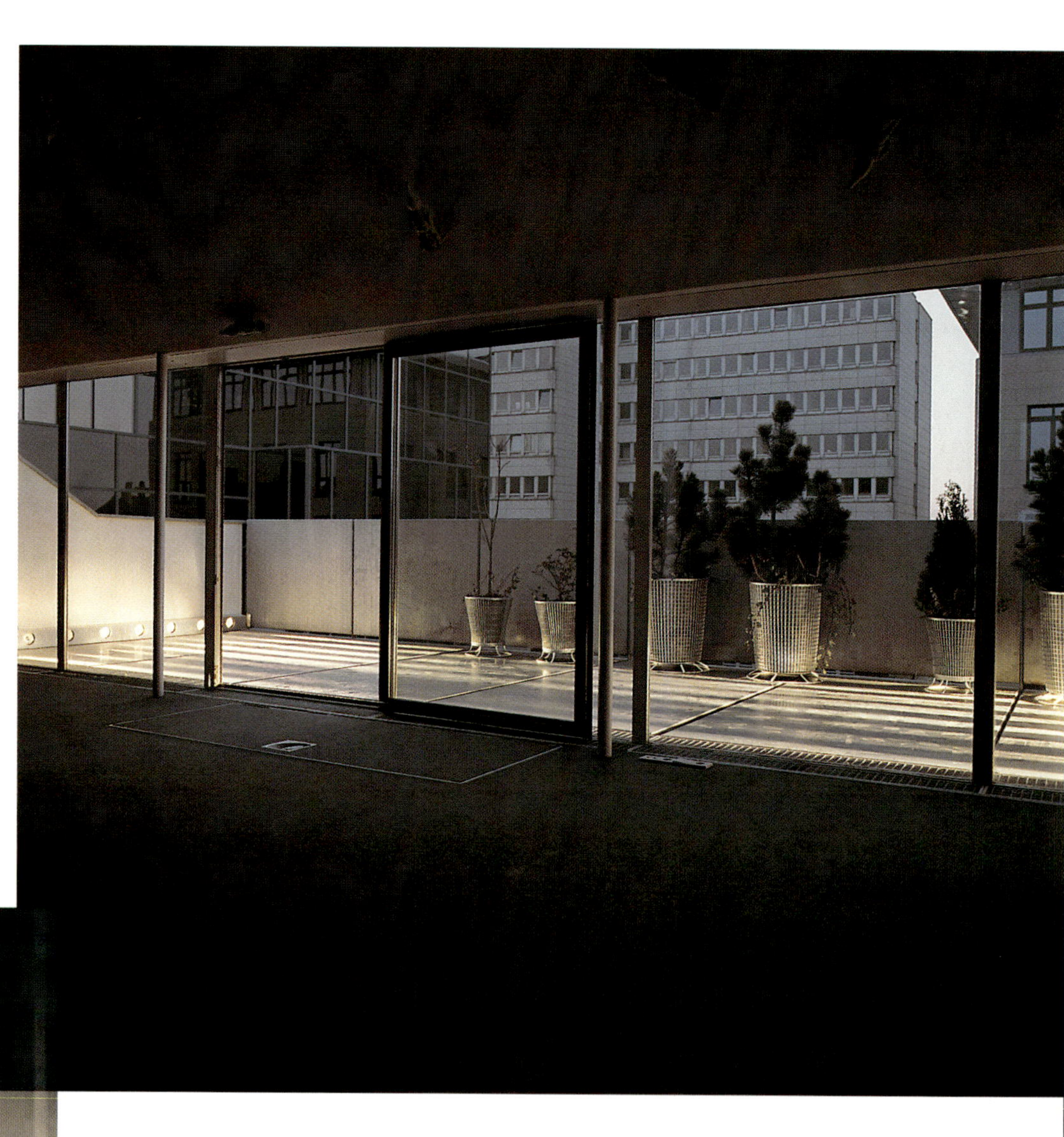

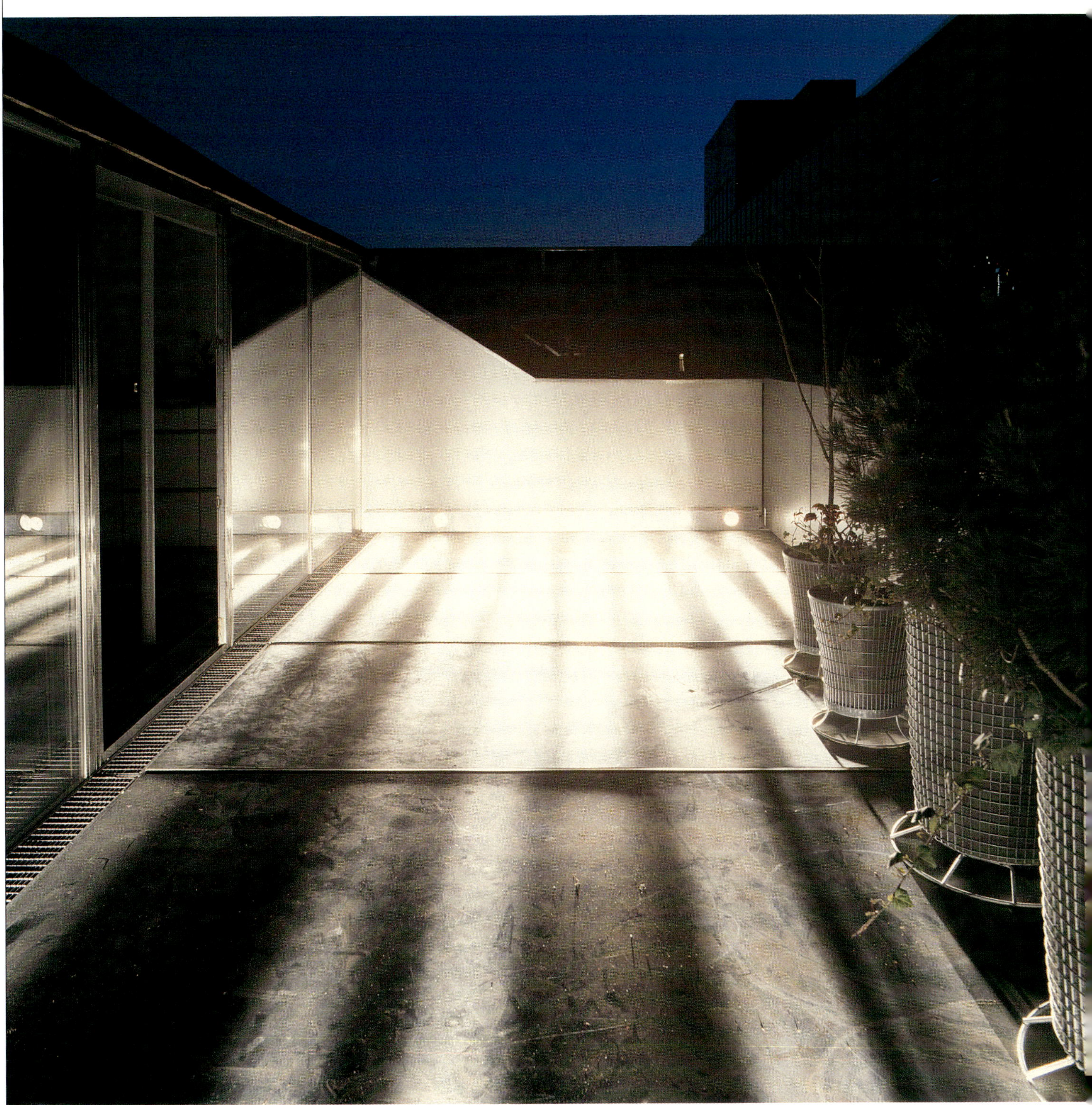

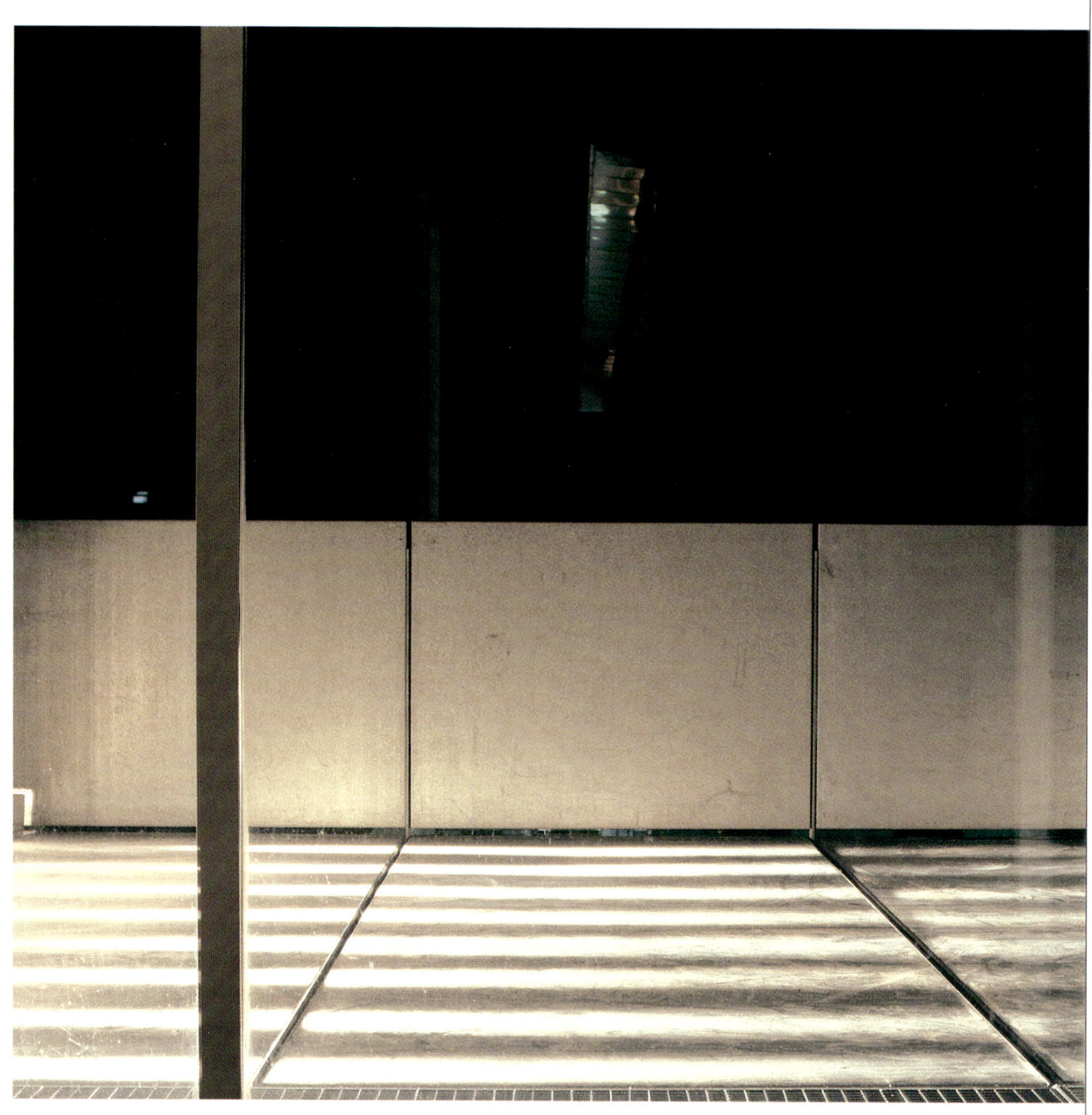

Eine Licht-Arbeit für einen Freund, der sich eine Lampe wünschte. Weil der Balkon des Appartments als Verlängerung des Innenraums geplant und gebaut wurde, entstand die Idee, „den Balkon anzuschalten". Das System besteht aus acht sich gegenüberliegenden Strahlern an den Schmalseiten des Balkons. Die Reflektionen auf dem Boden formen einen „Zebra-Teppich", der sich in ständiger Bewegung befindet. Jede der 16 Lampen ist mit einem zentralen Dimmer-System verbunden, das Länge, Geschwindigkeit und Intensität des einzelnen Dimm-Prozesses für jede Lampe bestimmt. Die Dimmer wiederum sind computergesteuert und verbunden mit einem Zufalls-Generator, der jedes Patterns zu einem unwiederholbaren macht.

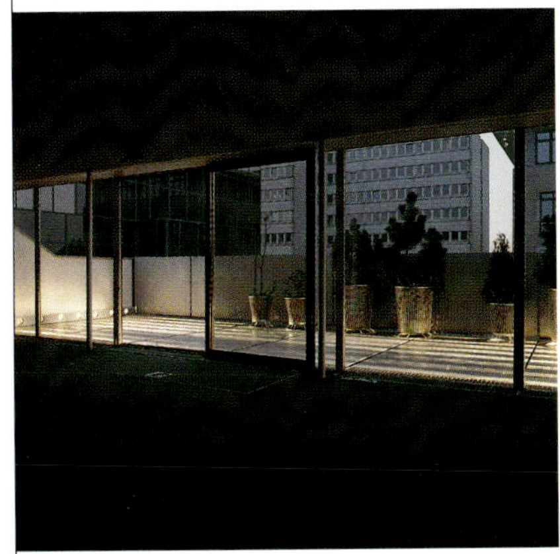

The facade photos show different stages of a light movement. The work consisted of light-tubes installed in nine windows of an apartment house (three on each floor). All nine windows were continually lit at about 20% light intensity. From time to time some of these were lit up to 100%. Different light patterns or movements could run as directed by a computer program. The pattern-structure ranged from fixed to random, with regard to both the composition as well as the intensity of movement. "Credible" light events, such as a lighting of a flat would alternate with "incredible" ones, such as fast moving successions. The time frame for the presentation of patterns and movements was about 30 seconds, because in this period a change of traffic lights in front of the building took place giving either pedestrians or motorists the chance to see one light "event". Concerning the incorporation of (digitally operated) rhythms into everyday-life, this project, of course, has implications to sonic systems.

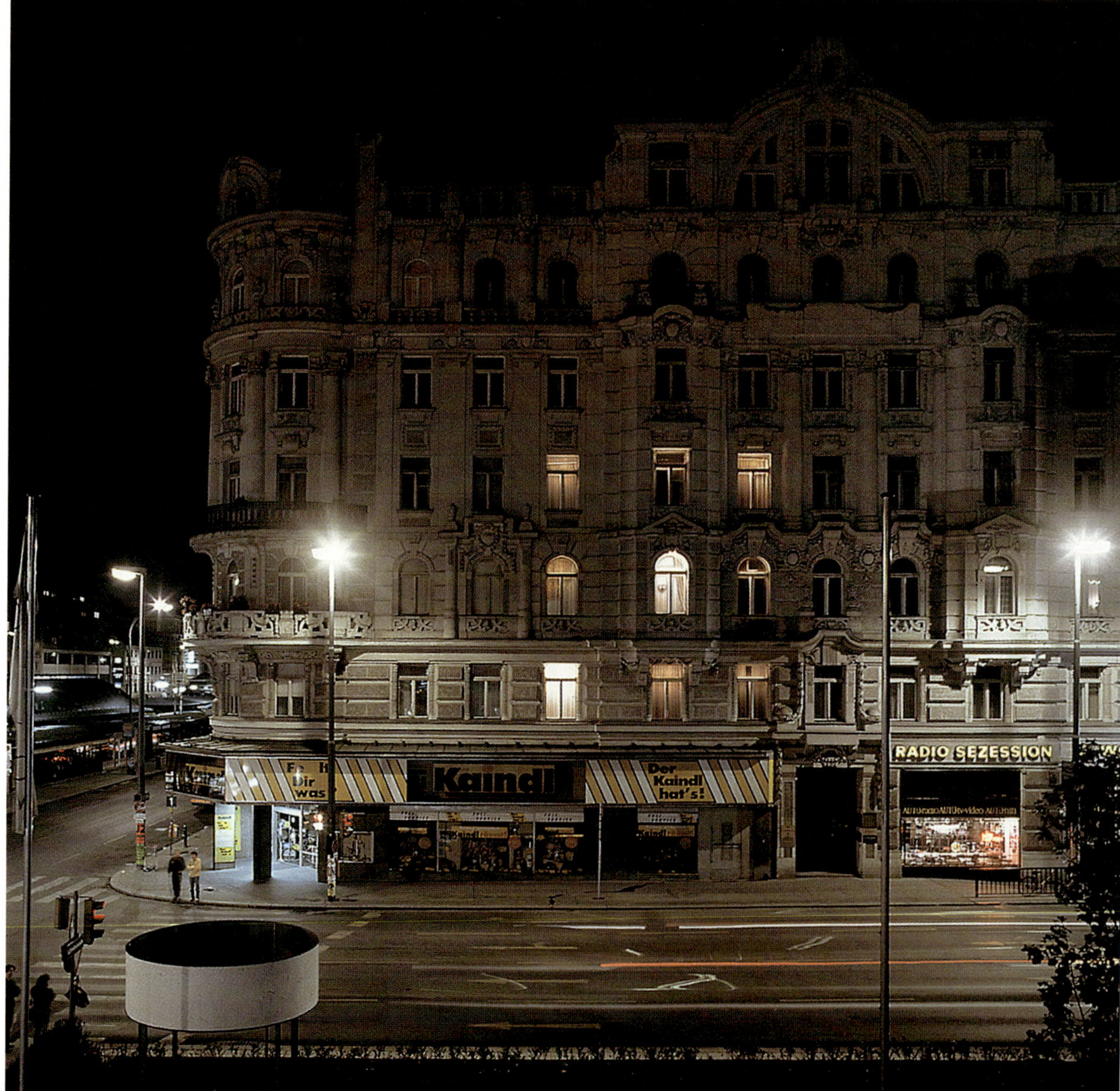

Die Photos der Fassade zeigen verschiedene Zustände einer Licht-Bewegung. Die Installation bestand aus Glühfaden-Langlampen, die in neun Fenstern (drei pro Stockwerk) eines Mietshauses angebracht waren. Alle Fenster waren konstant mit etwa 20% der verfügbaren Lichtintensität beleuchtet. Von einem Computer-Programm ange-steuert, konnten, durch Hochfahren der Lichtintensität einzelner Lampen, verschiedene Licht-Muster oder Bewe-gungen erzeugt werden. Die Muster-Bildung reichte von fest komponiert bis zu „ausgewürfelt" – und dies betraf sowohl die Komposition als auch die Bewegungs-Geschwindigkeit. Glaubwürdige Lichtsituationen, wie z.B. die Beleuchtung einer Wohnung, wechselten mit unwahrscheinlichen, wie Lauflicht-artigen Bewegungen. Die Zeit-Spanne für die Präsentation eines Muster- oder Bewegungs-Komplexes betrug ungefähr 30 Sekunden – in diesem Intervall wechselte die Ampelschaltung am Fuß des Gebäudes – somit hatten Fußgänger oder Autofahrer die Möglichkeit, zumindest jeweils ein „Ereignis" zu sehen. Die Eingliederung von (digital operierenden) Rhythmen in die Alltäglichkeit betreffend, hat dieses Projekt natürlich auch Auswirkungen auf Arbeiten mit Klang.

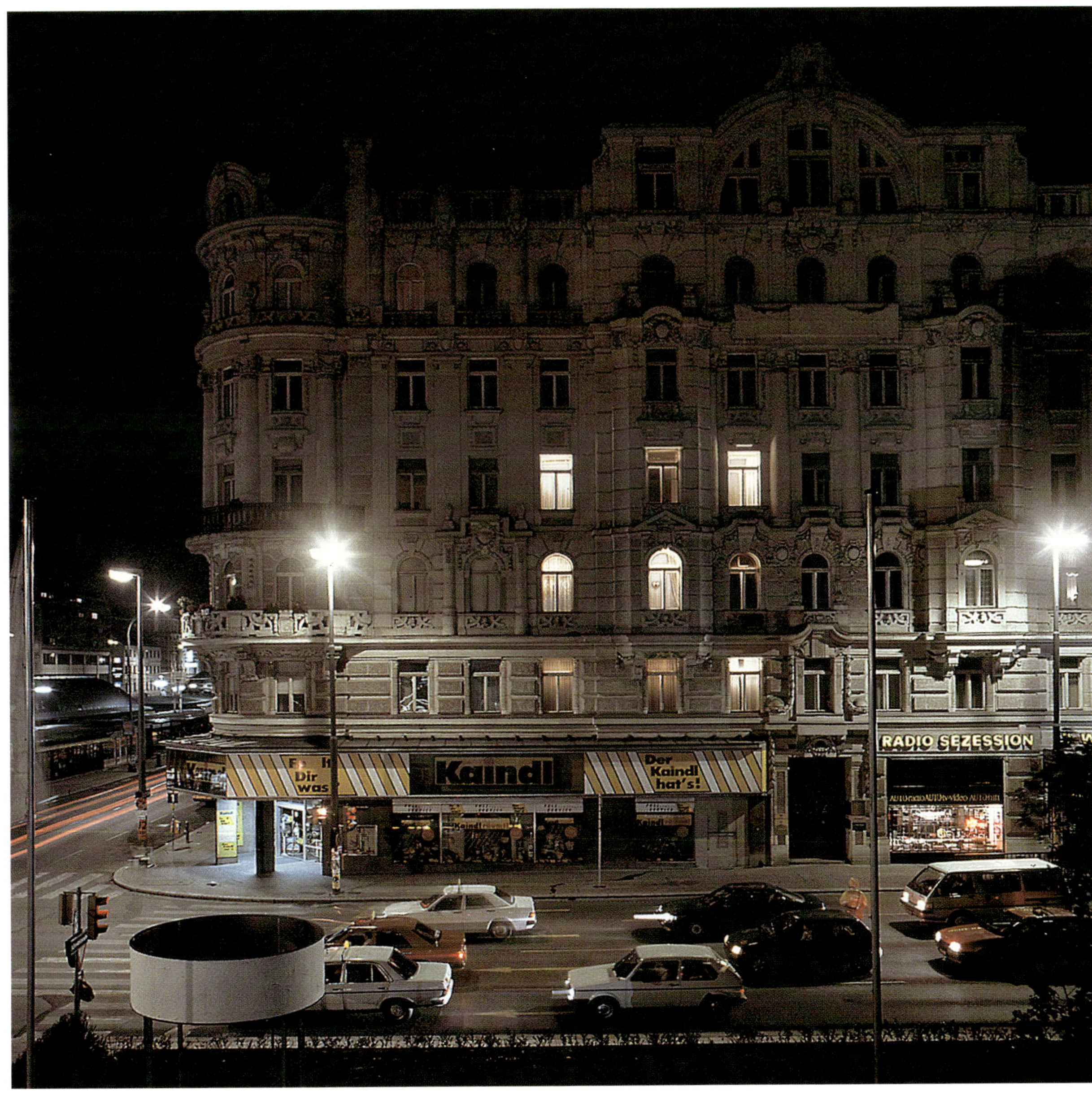

"**A composition** using the means of the theatre". A group of actors describes the audience, and develops -- at the same time -- methods to sonically and choreographically transform the resulting sentences and movements. This interaction between group and audience was combined with a "sound-scape" and a light system, both programmed and running on a compositional score, which allowed for independent emphasis of the surrounding space (in case of the Trier performance the entrance hall of a classical palace).

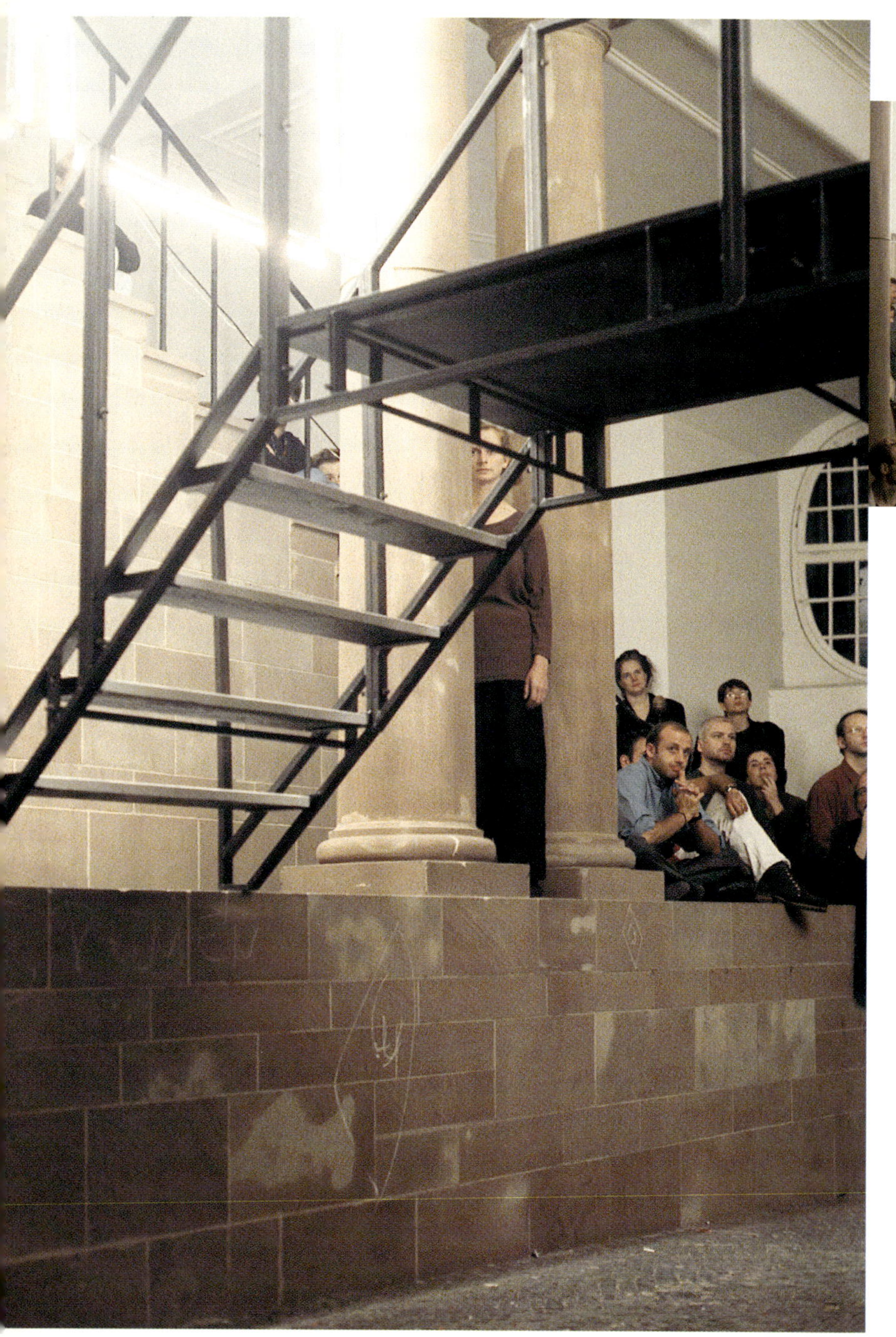

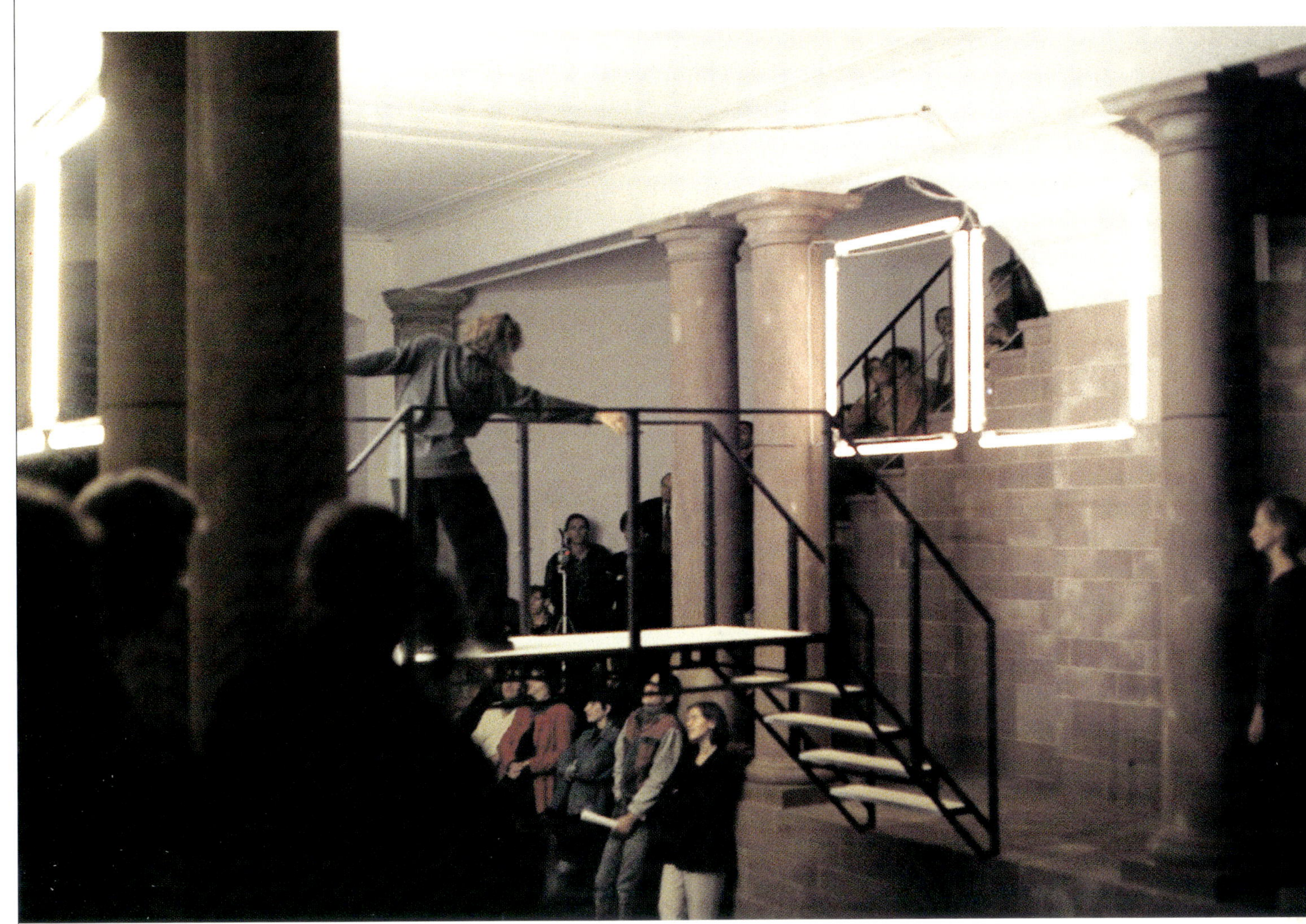

„Eine Komposition mit den Mitteln des Theaters". Eine Gruppe von Schaupielern (Akteuren) beschreibt die Zuhörerschaft und entwickelt – gleichzeitig – Methoden, die resultierenden Sätze und Bewegungen klanglich und choreographisch zu transformieren. Diese Interaktion zwischen einer Gruppe und einer Zuhörerschaft wurde kombiniert mit einer Klang- und Licht-Installation, beide programmiert und komponiert, was den Umraum zum gleichberechtigt aktivierten Teil der Performance machte.

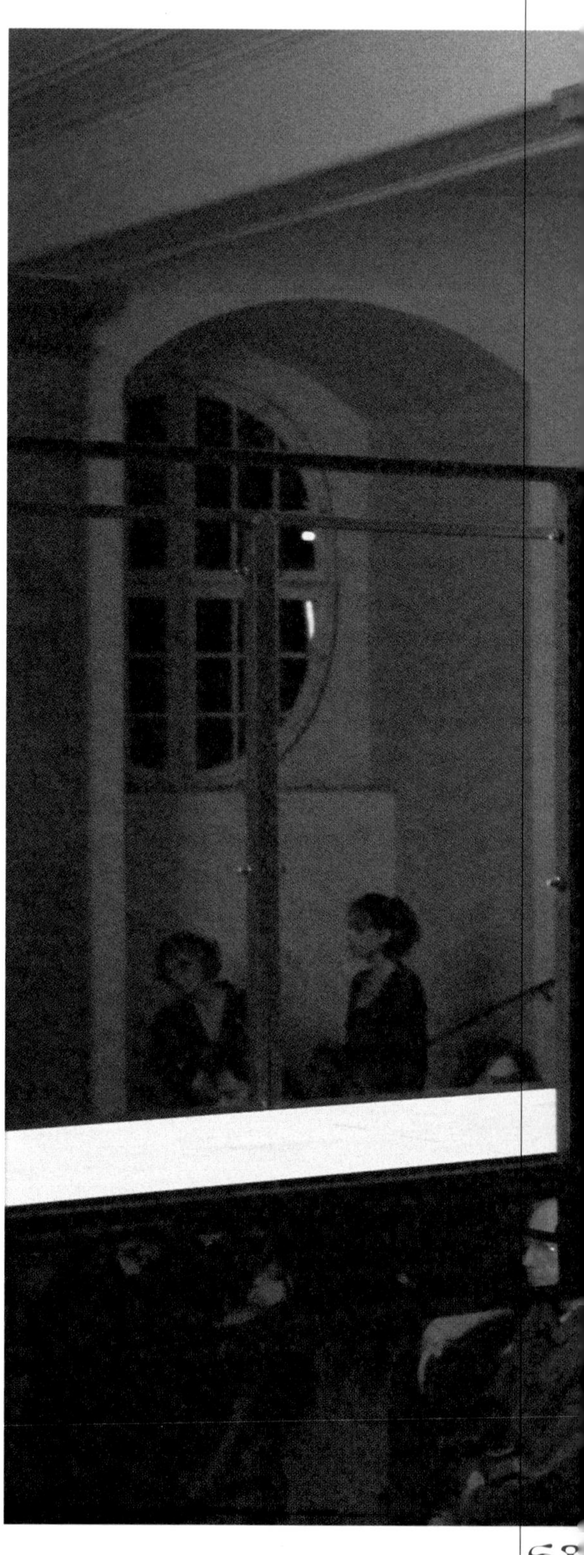

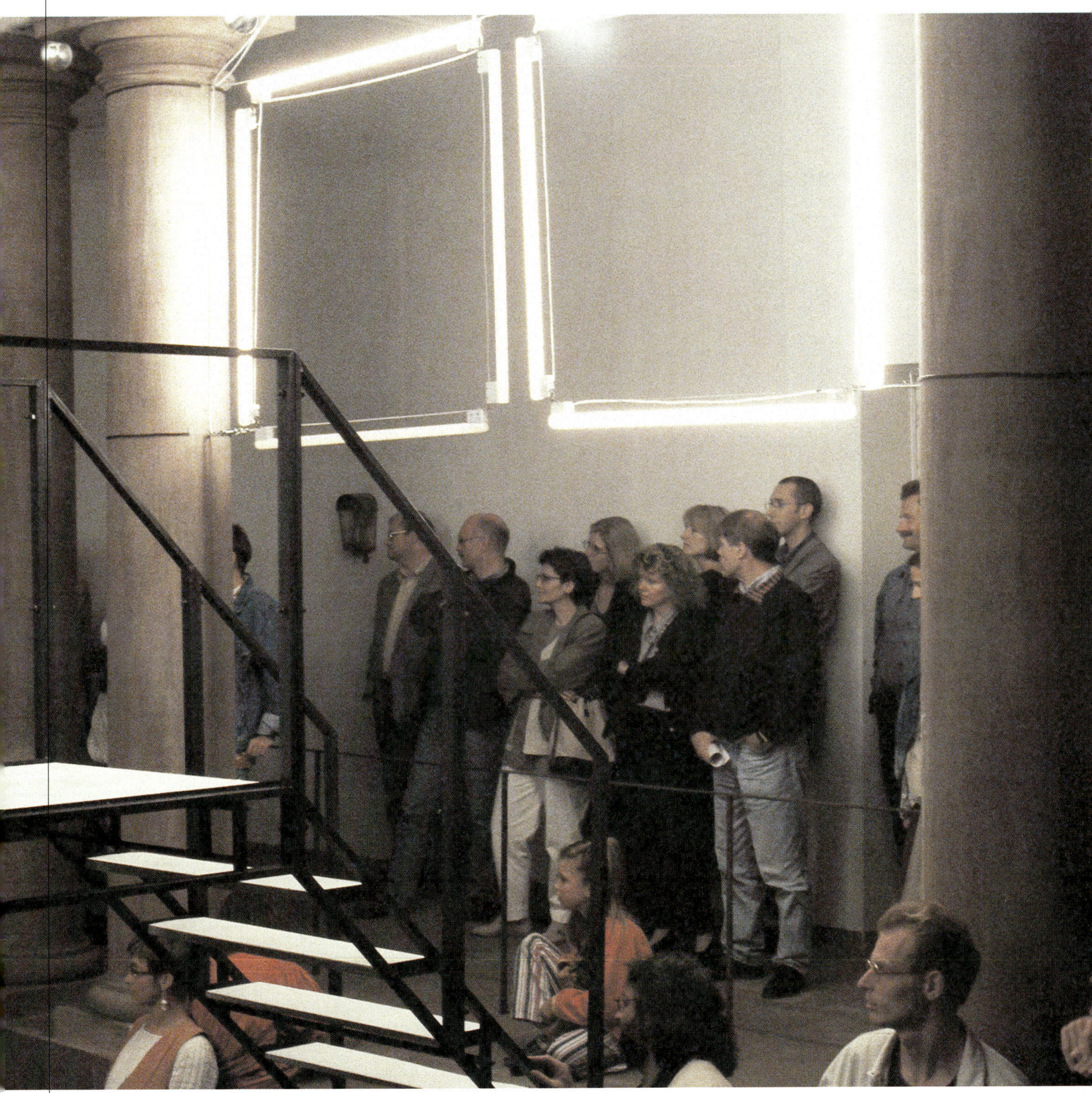

The construction of a transportable, flexible system that allows for site-specific sound-installations followed the line of thought that if an (electronically) reproduced sound sounds different in each environment, why not actually make this sonic environmental factor the exclusive source of sound... The "clapper"-system plays objects, rooms or spaces, according to the placement of the electronically driven "clappers" and the specific resonance of the materials and objects to which they are attached. The system consists of a computer program, an interface and several (min 16, max. 128) magnets, which can be independently operated with regard to both clapping speed and dynamics. During the first public performance of this system at Kawasaki City Museum as part of the "sonic perception" festival, the magnets were attached beneath the seats in the audience. The installations that followed (Seattle, San Francisco, Frankfurt a.M.) examined the sonic body of spaces or object-constellations of which we daily make use. The last version of the system is equipped with a real-time sound-transformation interface –– meaning the harmonic spectrum of sound events in spaces or places (voices or engine sounds for example) are recorded, analyzed and transformed into percussive patterns.

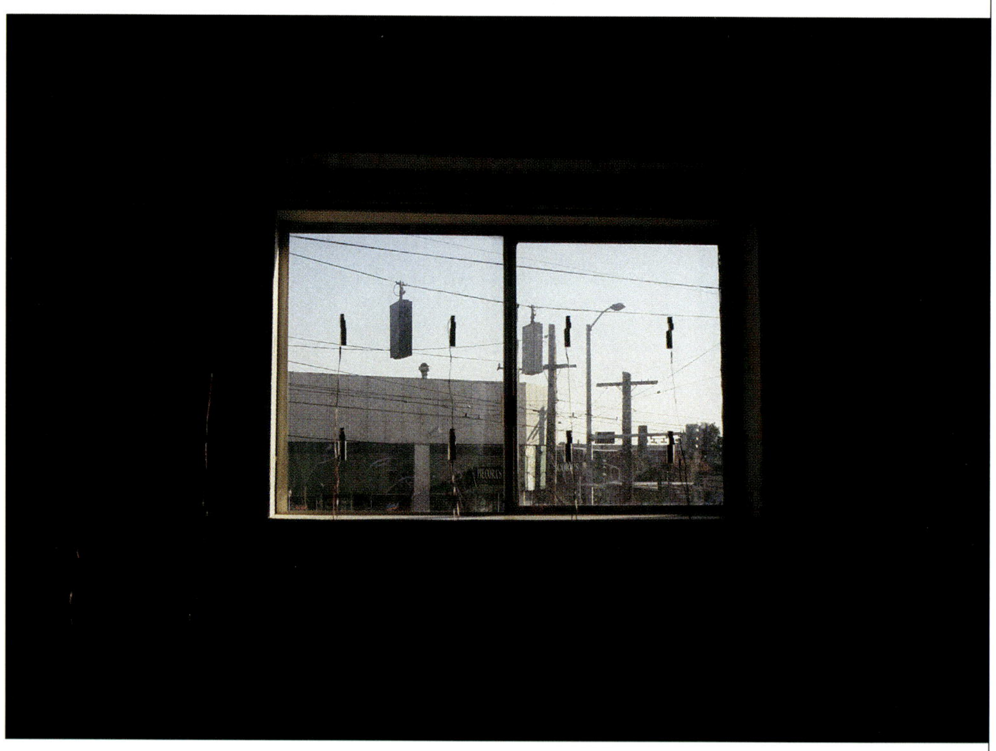

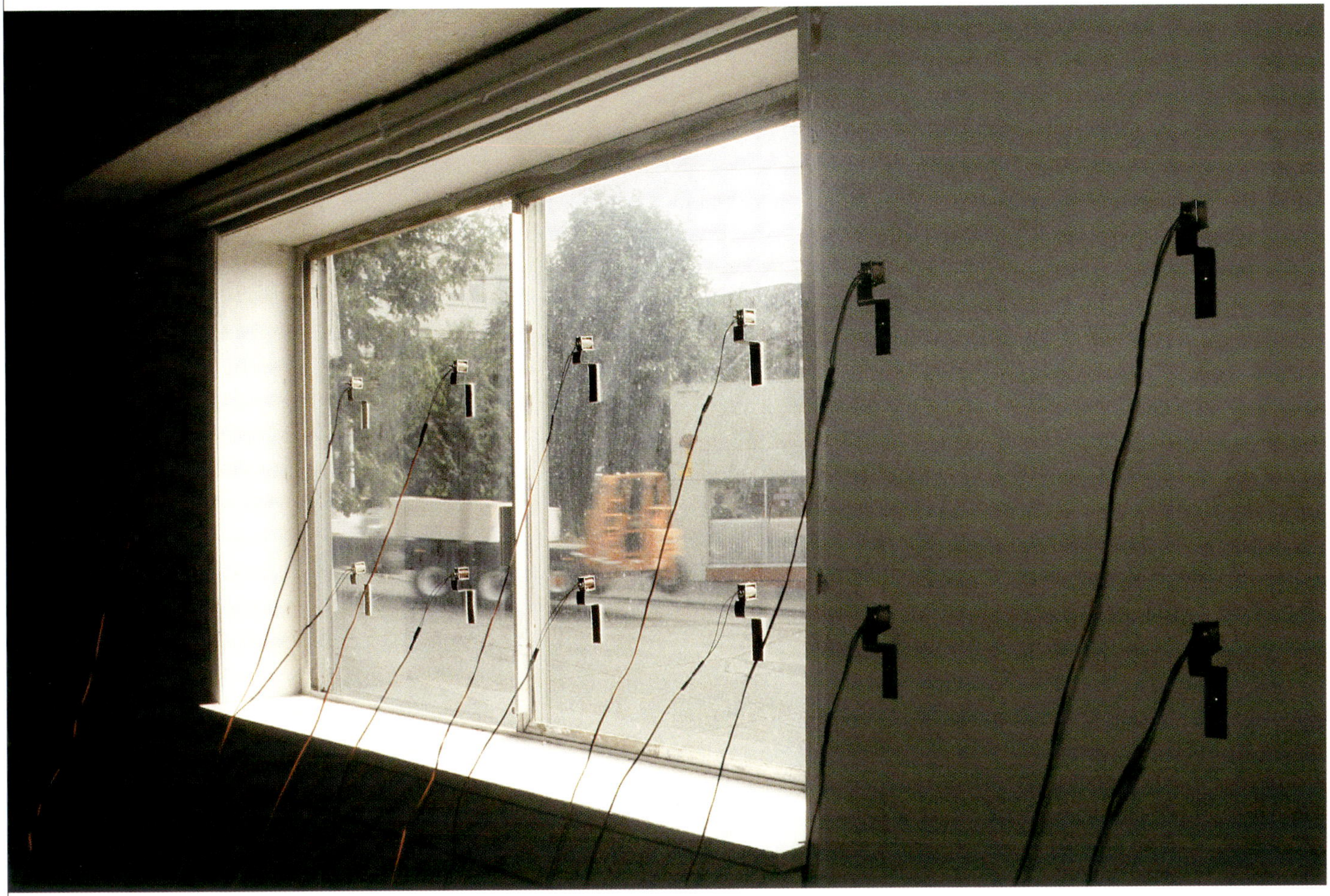

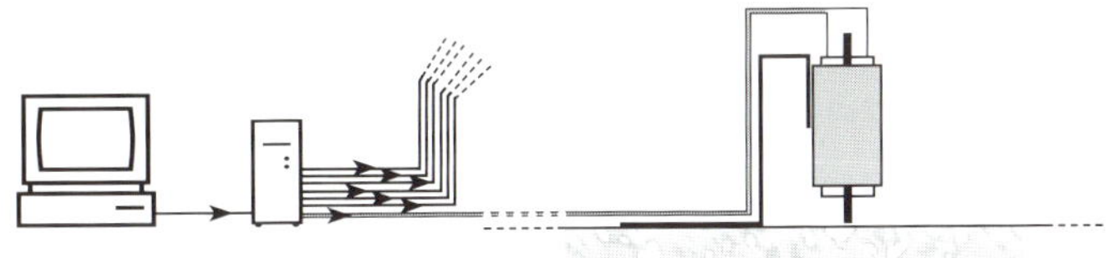

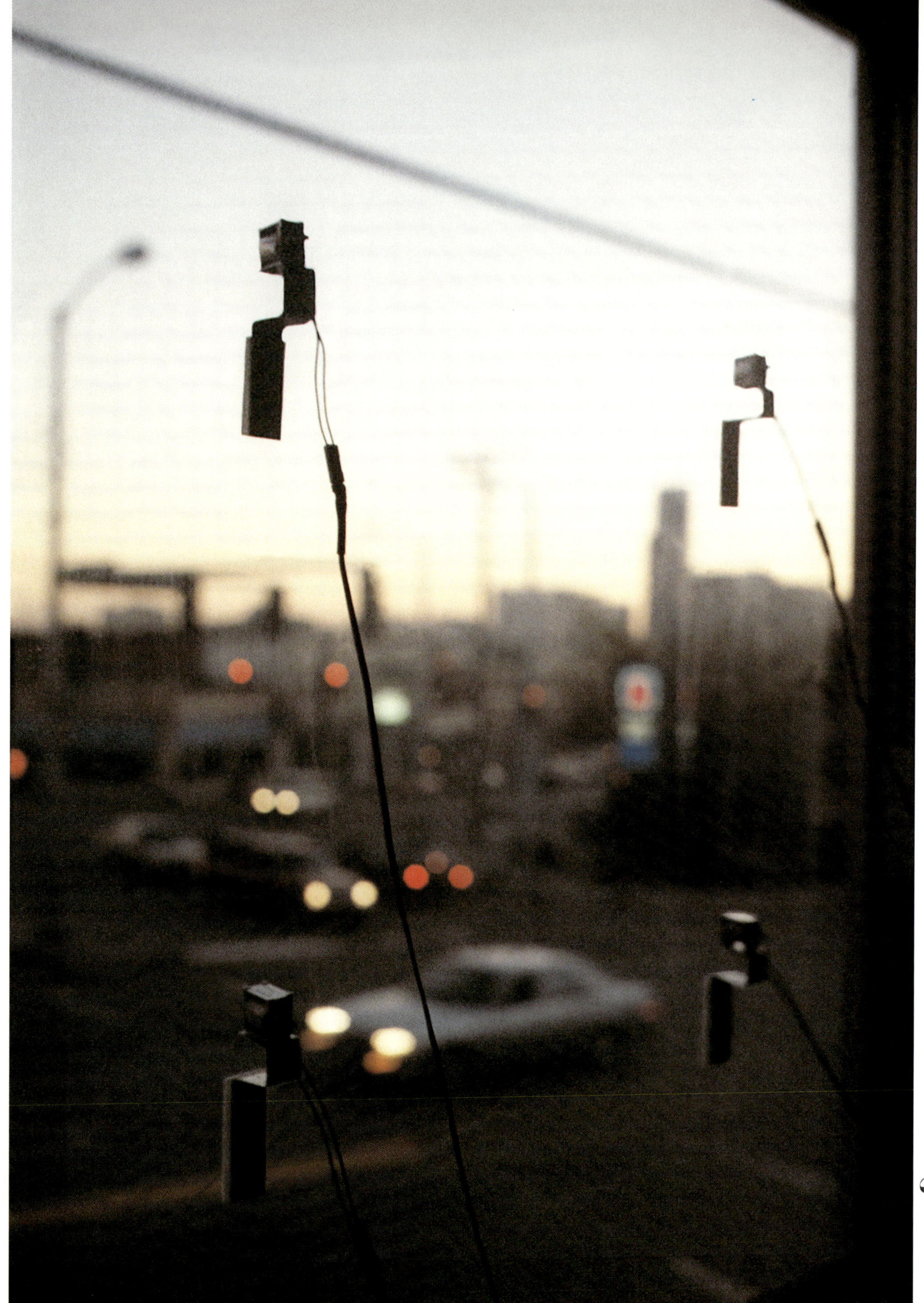

Wenn sich dieselben elektronisch reproduzierten Klänge in jedem Raum anders anhören: warum dann nicht diese Klang-Umgebungs-Differenz zum exklusiven Klangfaktor machen? Das war die Ausgangsfrage für die Entwicklung dieses transportablen, flexiblen Systems.

Das „Clapper" System „spielt" Gegenstände, Räume oder Plätze, je nachdem wie und wo die elektronisch gesteuerten Clapper angebracht sind, und wie die jeweils spezifische Resonanz der bespielten Materialien sich verhält. Es besteht aus einem Computer-Programm, einem Interface und einigen (mindestens 16, maximal 128) Hubmagneten, die unabhängig – Geschwindigkeit und Anschlags-Dynamik betreffend – angesteuert werden können. Während der ersten öffentlichen Vorführung im Kawasaki City Museum waren die Magnete unter den Sitzen der Zuhörer angebracht. Die folgenden Installationen untersuchten die klanglichen Eigenschaften von Räumen und Gegenständen des täglichen Gebrauchs. In der letzten Version ist das System mit einer real-time Klang-Transformations-Schnittstelle ausgerüstet, d.h. das harmonische Spektrum von Klangereignissen in Räumen oder auf Plätzen (z.B. Stimmen oder Motor-geräusche) wird aufgenommmen, analysiert und gleichzeitig in perkussive Patterns umgesetzt.

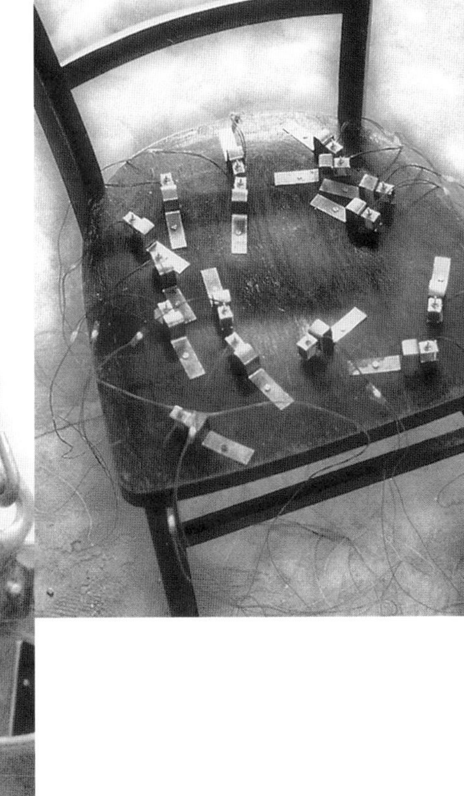

In the mid 90s one of my (perhaps unrealizable) fantasies was to create an invisible sculpture whose shape was only defined by its being void of sound (like a "flying cube" in a pedestrian zone...). This idea was fostered by the technically existing possibility of actually creating sonic "anti waves" via real time sound-analysis and digital signal-processing, which basically means muting a sound by inverting its wave-spectrum and emitting this inverted signal in real-time. What can be accomplished for cars or airplanes cannot (at least not today) be done in an open space since, with regard to both sound sources and listeners, the changes of the noise profile are far too rapid and complex. Nevertheless the idea to feed a transformed signal back into its source remained... The sound installation in Kunitachi in October of 1996 transformed a public space through sound. Eight microphones suspended over a suburban shopping street continuously recorded the noise of the cars passing. Each of the microphone's signals was analysed by a computer(program) which transformed the recorded noise into musically identifiable structures (sine-wave-clusters). When a car was passing on the one side, the pedestrian on the sidewalk heard the transformed and amplified signal from the other. Thus, not only was sound implanted into its noisy source, but also a sound passage was created in which the parameters for a composition related to both the movement of the different sound-sources and to a changing group of listeners.

Während der 90er Jahre war eine meiner (wahrscheinlich nie umsetzbaren) Ideen, eine unsichtbare Skulptur zu realisieren, deren Form nur durch ihre Lautlosigkeit definiert wird (zum Beispiel ein schwebender Kubikmeter „Stille" in einer Fußgängerzone). Die Idee wurde angeregt durch die tatsächlich bestehende Möglichkeit, mittels real-time Klang-Analyse und digitaler Klang Umwandlung „Gegen-Wellen" zu einem Geräusch zu erzeugen und dieses dadurch stark zu dämpfen (was durch Inversion des jeweiligen Wellenspektrums und zeitgleiche Ausstrahlung dieses Klangs erreicht wird). Was nun aber für Autos und Flugzeuge (in Grenzen) machbar ist, überfordert, auf den öffentlichen Raum angewandt, sowohl Klang-Analyse als auch Umrechnung: denn sowohl die Klangquellen als auch die Hörer betreffend, sind die Klang-Profile zu komplex und viel zu schnell wechselnd. Nichtsdestotrotz hielt sich die Idee, ein transformiertes Signal in seine Quelle zurückzuschicken...

Die Klanginstallation in Kunitachi im Oktober 1996 transformierte einen öffentlichen Raum durch Klang. Acht Mikrophone, die über einer Geschäftsstraße in Tokyo angebracht waren, nahmen die Geräusche der vorbeifahrenden Kraftfahrzeuge auf. Jedes der aufgenommen Geräusch-Spektren wurde von einem Computer(-Programm) analysiert und in identifizierbare musikalische Strukturen übersetzt (Sinus-Ton Reihen). Fuhr ein Auto auf der einen Seite an ihm vorbei, konnte ein Fußgänger den transformierten Klang auf der anderen hören. So wurde nicht nur Klang in seine geräuschhafte Quelle implantiert, sondern auch ein Stück

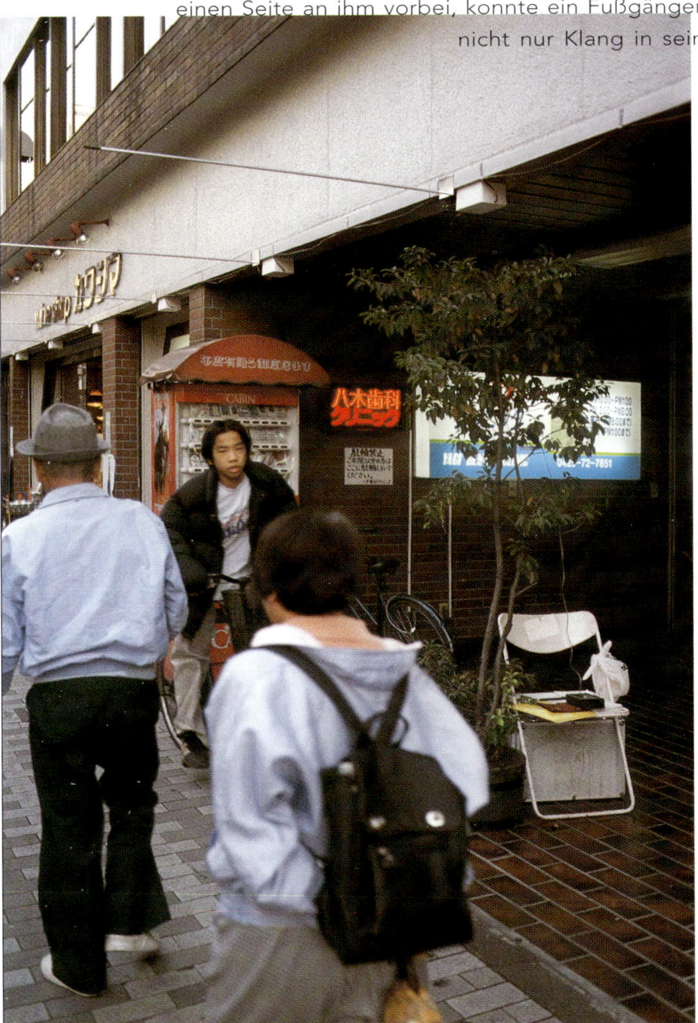

Weg gestaltet, in dem die Parameter für eine Komposition sowohl auf die verschiedenen Klangquellen als auch auf die sich verändernde Gruppe von Hörern Bezug nahmen.

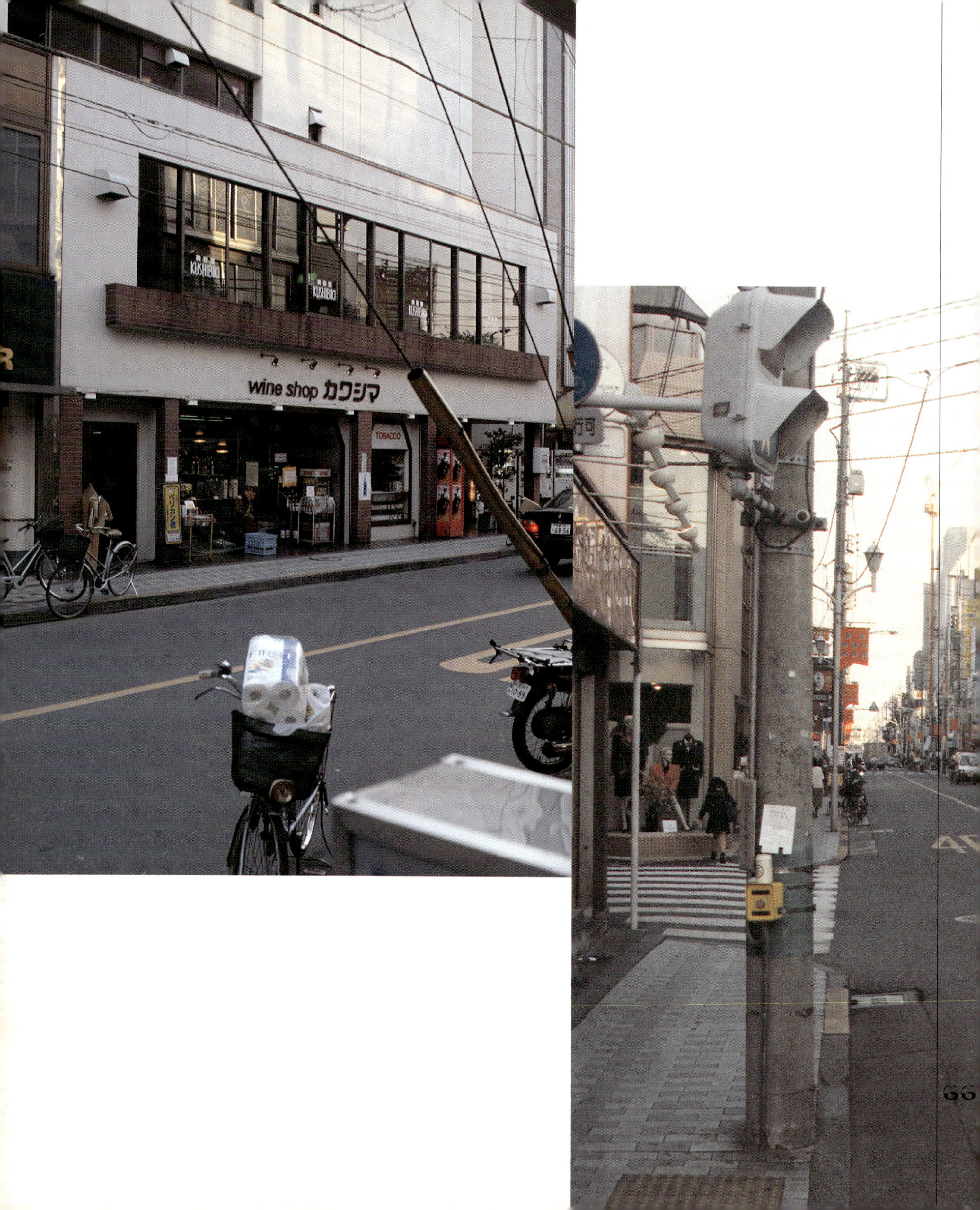

KUSHIBIKI
wine shop カワシマ
TOBACCO

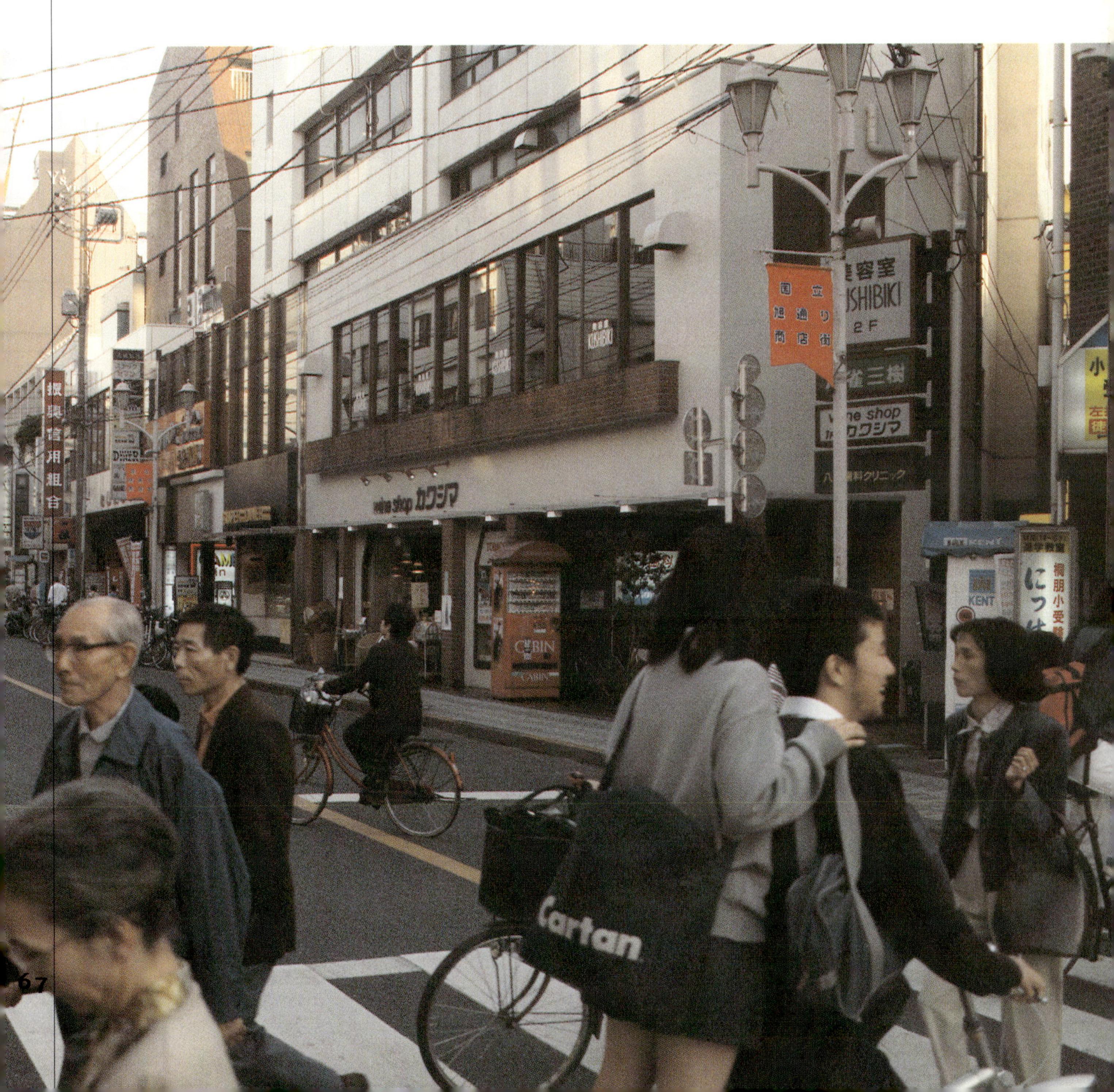

美容室
KUSHIBIKI
2 F
国立
旭通り
商店街
wine shop カクシマ
wine shop カワシマ
KUSHIBIKI
八王子科クリニック
KENT
KENT
CABIN
CABIN
cartan
DINER
小学
桐朋小受験
にっけ
進学教室

The system replaced the 60's glass-brick-wall between the old building and the annex. A reflective glass coating, developed for this project, together with an indirect lighting make the single glass pane an evenly lit "light-surface". Two different concepts are combined. Firstly the glass itself becomes the "light-source" –– translucent at daytime, lucent at night. Secondly, a "light-composition" accompanies the movement in the staircase –– human movement is translated into a correlative light-movement. Through (sensor) motion-control and a computer directed interface the light-parameters: duration, intensity, variation and attack can be used as independent compositional elements for each of the 15 panes of the "staircase window", thus producing variing sequences of light-movement.

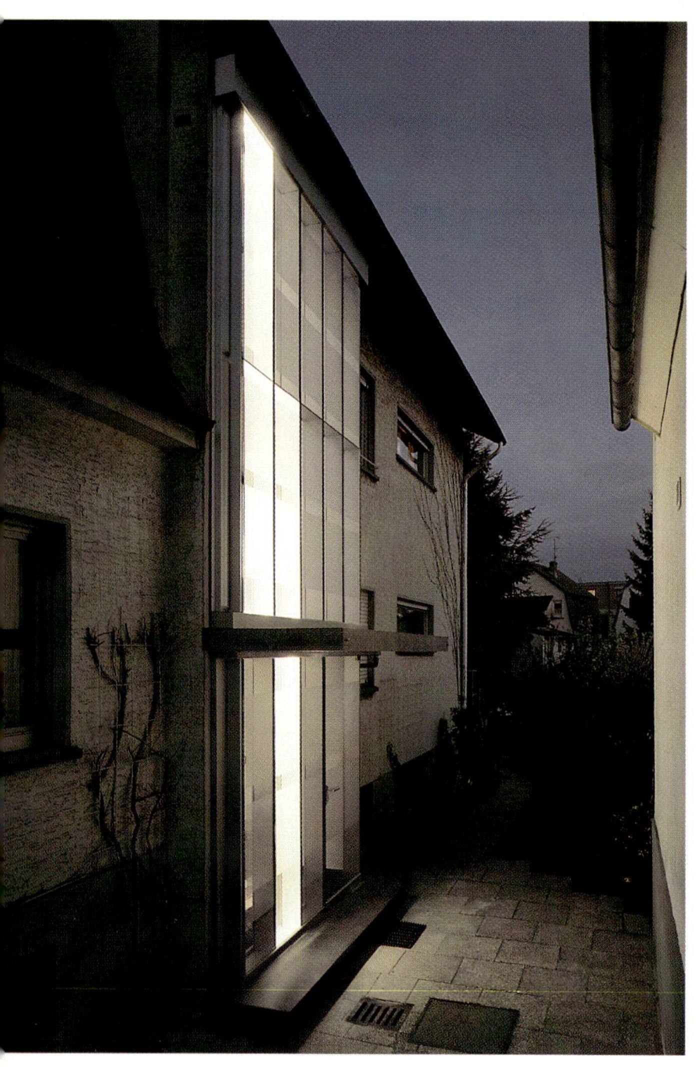
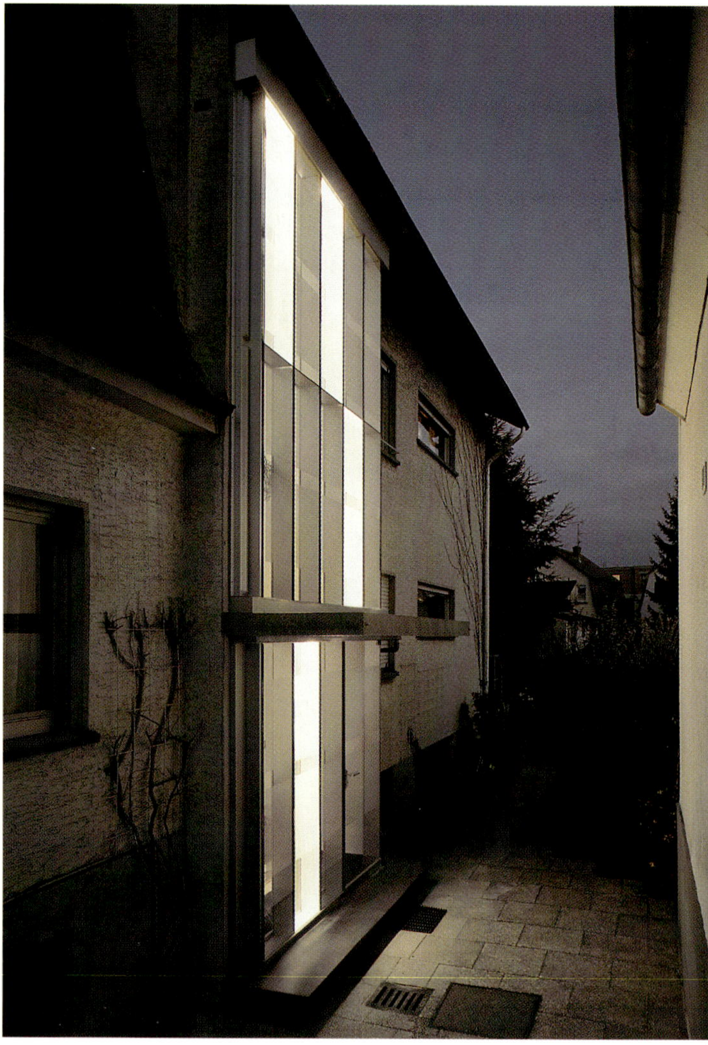

Das Treppenhaus-Fenster ersetzte eine 60er Jahre Glasbaustein-Wand zwischen dem alten Haus im Vordergrund und dem Anbau. Eine reflektierende Glasbeschichtung, die für dieses Projekt zusammen mit einer speziellen Leuchte entwickelt wurde, macht aus einer einzelnen Glasscheibe eine gleichmäßig leuchtende Fläche. Zwei verschiedene Konzepte werden verbunden: zum einem wird das Glas selbst zur Leuchtquelle, durchsichtig bei Tag, leuchtend bei Nacht; zum anderen entsteht eine „Licht-Komposition" auf der Glasfront: die Bewegungen der Menschen im Treppenhaus werden in ko-relative Bewegungen des Lichts übersetzt. Durch Bewegungs-Melder und ein computergesteuertes Interface können die Parameter – Dauer, Intensität, Variation und Dimm-Geschwindigkeit – für jedes der 15 Segmente des Treppenhaus-Fensters unabhängig bestimmt werden und somit stets variierende Lichtsequenzen erzeugen.

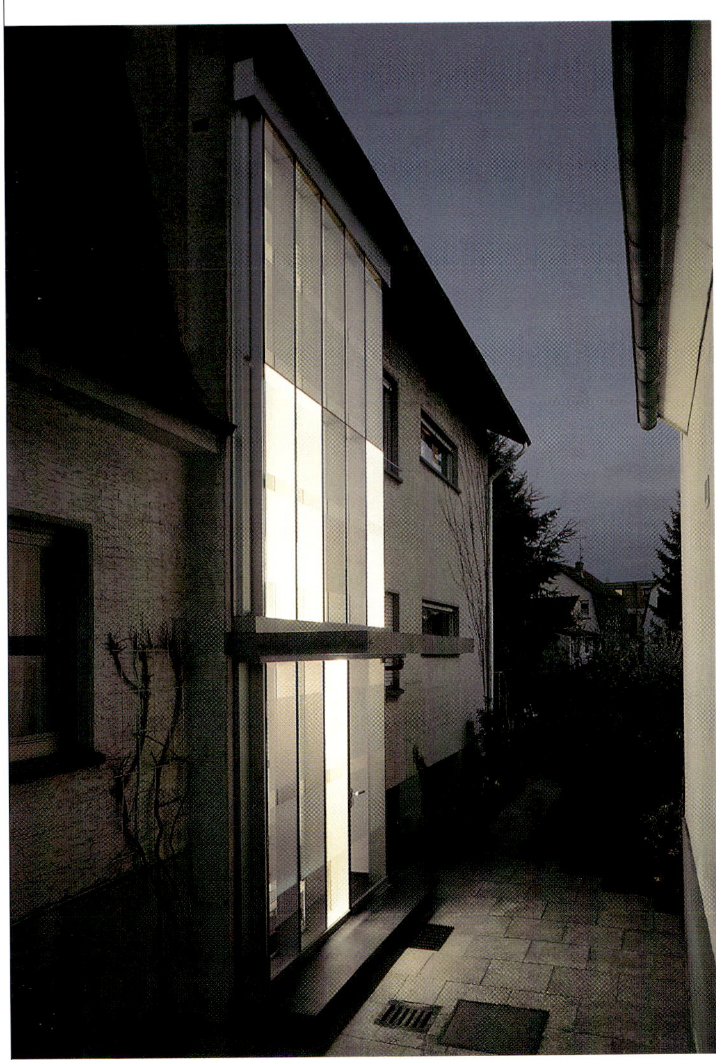

The **Light-net intersects** the center of the entrance hall at the Fachhochschule (Technical University) Frankfurt a.M.. Its function is only triggered if the onlooker acts. Voices or movement, if connected with sound, generate impulses: moving patterns consisting of diversely pulsating, flashing light sequences accompany or mirror the movement of the sounds. In this case light doesn't illuminate, it defines the status of a light-composition with reference to its trigger. At the same time the light becomes a trigger itself: as soon as the movement, seeing its sonic impulse mirrored in moving lights on the system, becomes reflexive, it will change and so will its transformation on the net. Space thus becomes an interface, a 3D input for information —— intersected by a screen, which feeds the output of the transformed information back to the input. The programming of the system has two references. On one hand there are the conditions of the feedback as a necessary introduction to an understanding of the system: the onlooker identifies events on the net as originated by his actions. On the other hand —— to avoid an overly obvious stressing of analogies —— an autonomous form-generating program is implemented.

A microphone is installed on both ends of the net. A parallel recording and a running time comparison allows for the localization of sound-events in space. Because the net reproduces the space's dimensions, reduced in scale, a light-event on the net can define the spot in which the sound is occuring and, if the sound-source is moving, accompany it. Because program and interface work in real-time, sound and light act in synchronicity. If several sounds overlap —— if, say, a group of students takes a break in the hall —— the program searches for the most dominant sound-signal: here dynamics, melody, or sonic difference can serve as a criterion for discretion. While comparing similarity or difference the program can relate several signal sources at the same time: co-ordinated or overlapping patterns will result. Only as an exception will light-events consist of single flashes —— instead patterns will be generated whose shape and movement are oriented toward dynamics, dispersion, volatility, rhythm, or dominance —— here the borders between illustrating, accompanying and self-referring, abstract patterns change fleeetingly. The basic stimulus-response-function does not prevail. According to the frequency of reactions, inter-ruptions may occur or the system may enter a phase of stillness. The goal is to avoid repetition on both levels: interactive periods and generated patterns interchange to create an equilibrium of variations.

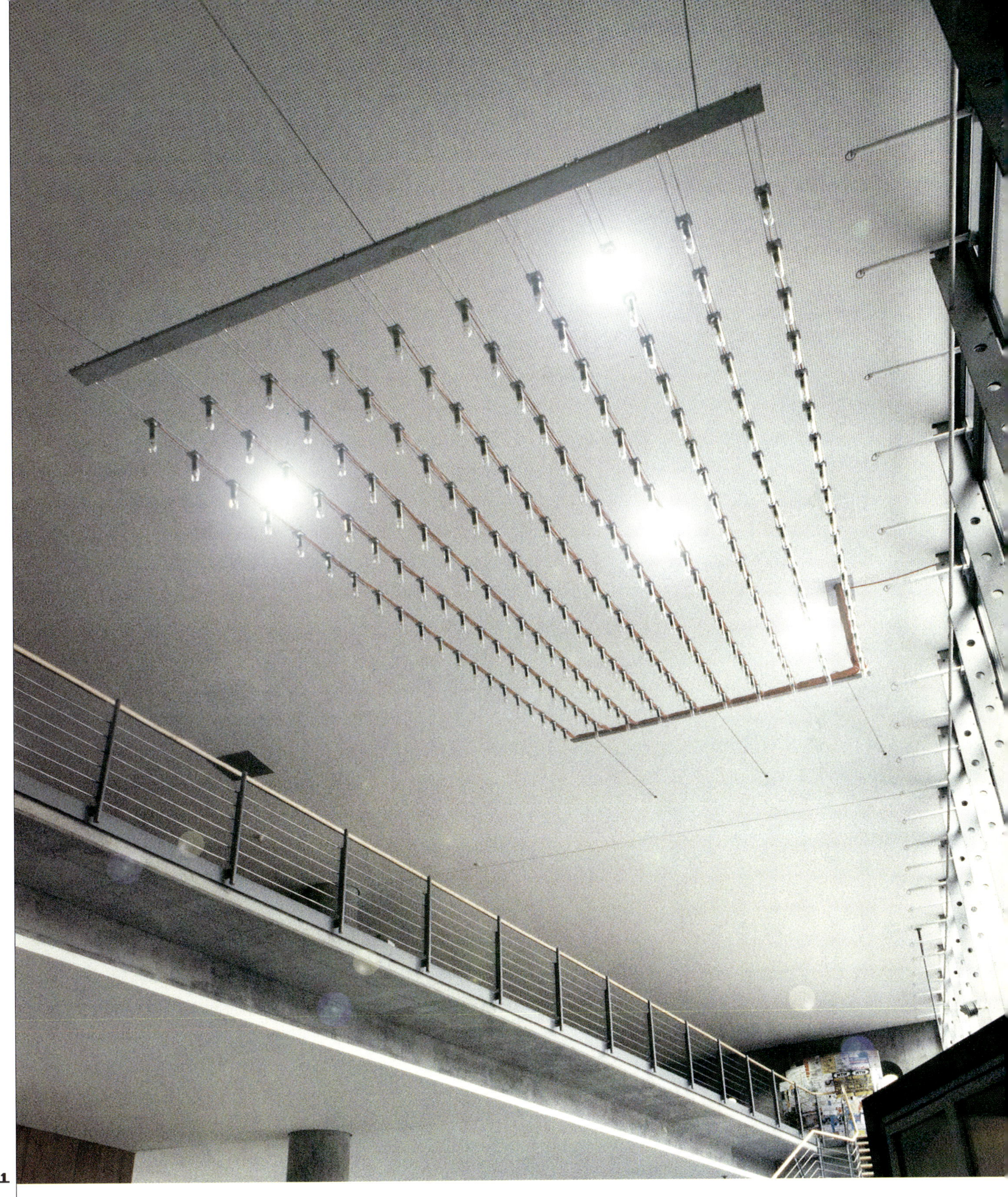

Das Lichtnetz hängt in der Mitte der Eingangshalle der FH Frankfurt a.M. Die Funktion wird nur dann aktiviert, wenn der Betrachter agiert. Stimmen oder Bewegungen oder andere klangerzeugende Aktionen generieren Impulse: bewegte Muster, bestehend aus verschieden pulsierenden Blitz-Licht Sequenzen begleiten oder spiegeln die Bewegung der Klänge. In diesem Fall beleuchtet Licht nicht – es definiert den Status einer Licht-Komposition in bezug auf ihren Auslöser. Aber das Licht wird gleichermaßen zum Auslöser: sobald ein „Betrachter" (d.h. eine Klangquelle) seine „outputs" auf dem Licht-Netz gespiegelt sieht und sich reflexiv verhält, wird er seine Bewegung ggfs. verändern und damit auch wiederum die Transformation auf dem Netz. Raum wird solchermaßen zu einem dreidimensionalen Interface; durchschnitten von einem Schirm (dem Netz), der den Output der transformierten Information wieder an den Input zurückgibt.

Die Programmierung des Netzes hat zwei Bezugspunkte: einerseits formuliert es die Bedingungen der Rückkopplung als notwendige Einführung in ein Verstehen des Systems – der Betrachter identifiziert die Ereignisse im Netz als von ihm verursacht; andererseits – um eine offensichtliche Überstrapazierung von Analogien zu vermeiden – ist ein autonom Form-gestaltendes Programm implementiert.

An beiden Enden des Netzes ist ein Mikrophon installiert. Eine permanente Aufnahme mit parallelem Zeitabgleich erlaubt es, Klang-Ereignisse zu orten. Weil das Netz den Dimensionen des Raums in verkleinertem Maßstab entspricht, kann ein Blitz-Licht Ereignis auf dem Netz den Ort eines Klang-Ereignisses bezeichnen und falls der Klang sich bewegt, ihn begleiten. Da Programm und Interface in Echtzeit arbeiten, besteht zwischen Klang und Licht Synchronizität. Falls sich mehrere Klänge überlagern – wenn sich zum Beispiel mehrere Studenten in der Halle aufhalten – sucht das Programm nach dem markantesten Signal: Lautstärke, Melodizität oder Differenz können als Kriterien für eine Auswahl fungieren. Während es Ähnlichkeit oder Differenz zwischen den einzelnen Klangquellen vergleicht, kann das Programm mehrere Signale zueinander in Beziehung setzen: koordinierte oder sich überlappende Patterns resultieren. Nur ausnahmsweise bestehen Licht-Events aus einzelnen Blitzen – stattdessen werden Patterns erzeugt, die in Form und Bewegung sich an Lautstärke, Verteilung, Flüchtigkeit, Rhythmus oder Dominanz orientieren – hier sind die Grenzen zwischen illustrierenden, begleitenden und selbstbezüglich abstrakten Patterns fließend. Die grundsätzliche Stimulus-Response-Funktion behält hierbei nicht die Oberhand. Je nach Frequenz der Reaktionen können Pausen die Funktion unterbrechen, oder eine Phase der Stille auslösen. Ziel ist, Wiederholung auf beiden Ebenen zu vermeiden: interaktive Perioden und generierte Patterns wechseln sich ab, um ein Equilibrium von Variationen zu erzeugen.

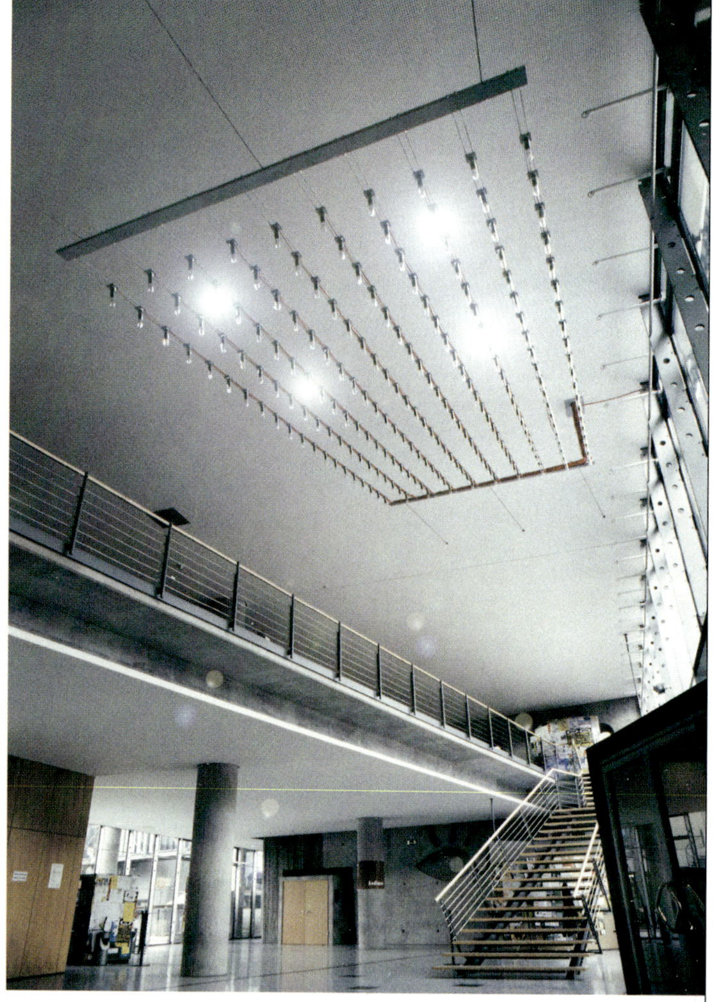

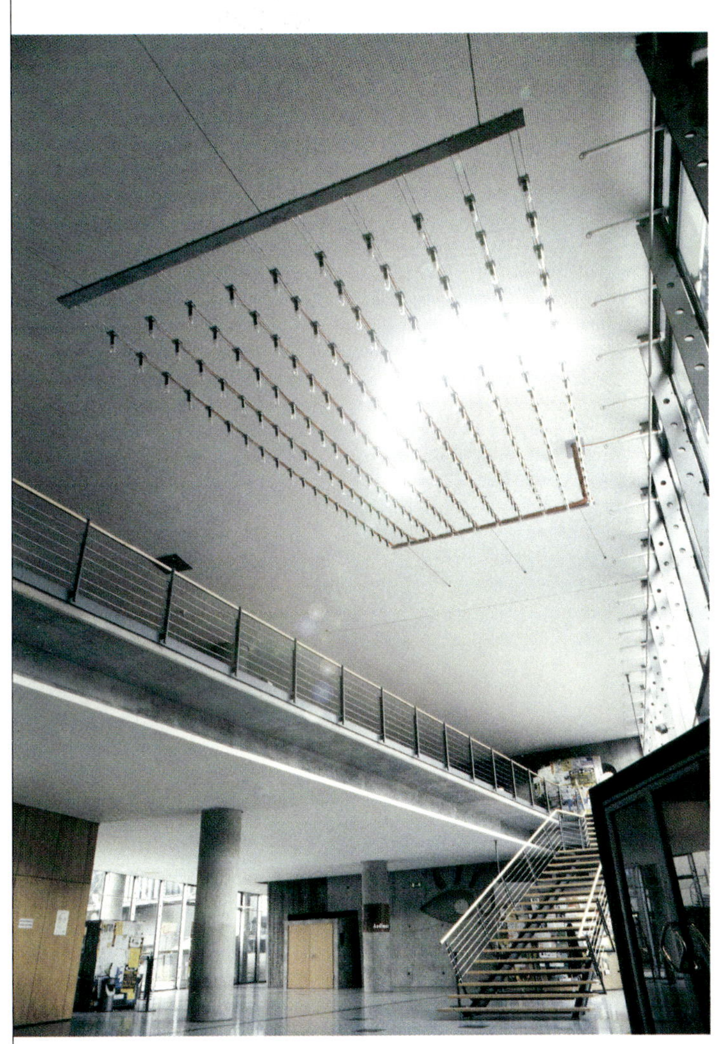

The idea is actually to arrive at something like a sonic "companion" –– a cigarette box-sized kit one carries around while –– according to the selected program –– it transforms environmental sounds into parallel sonic structures. As a prototype for this marketable small kit the present semi-stationary transformer was developed at the beginning of 1997 (it can also run on battery-power, but is still fairly large...). Built in an edition of 10 it transfers the experiences gained from the Kunitachi-project to a programming which can flexibly react to changing sonic inputs –– for example, after a certain amount of repetitions it switches program-levels, or -differentiation.

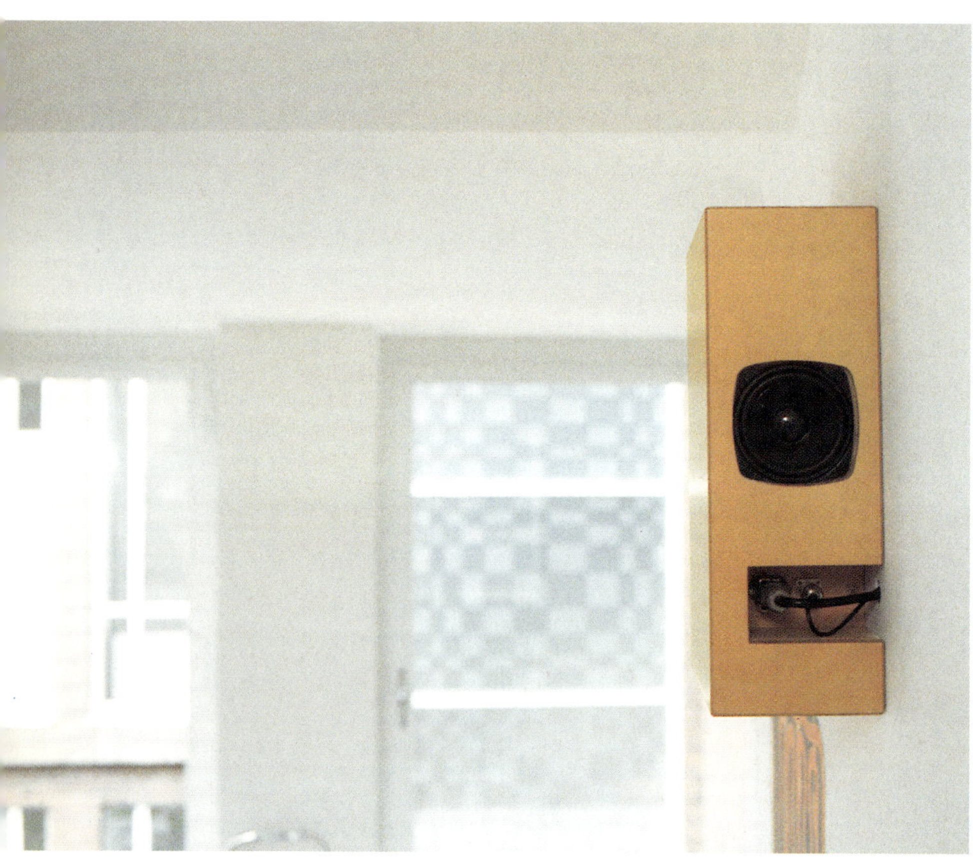

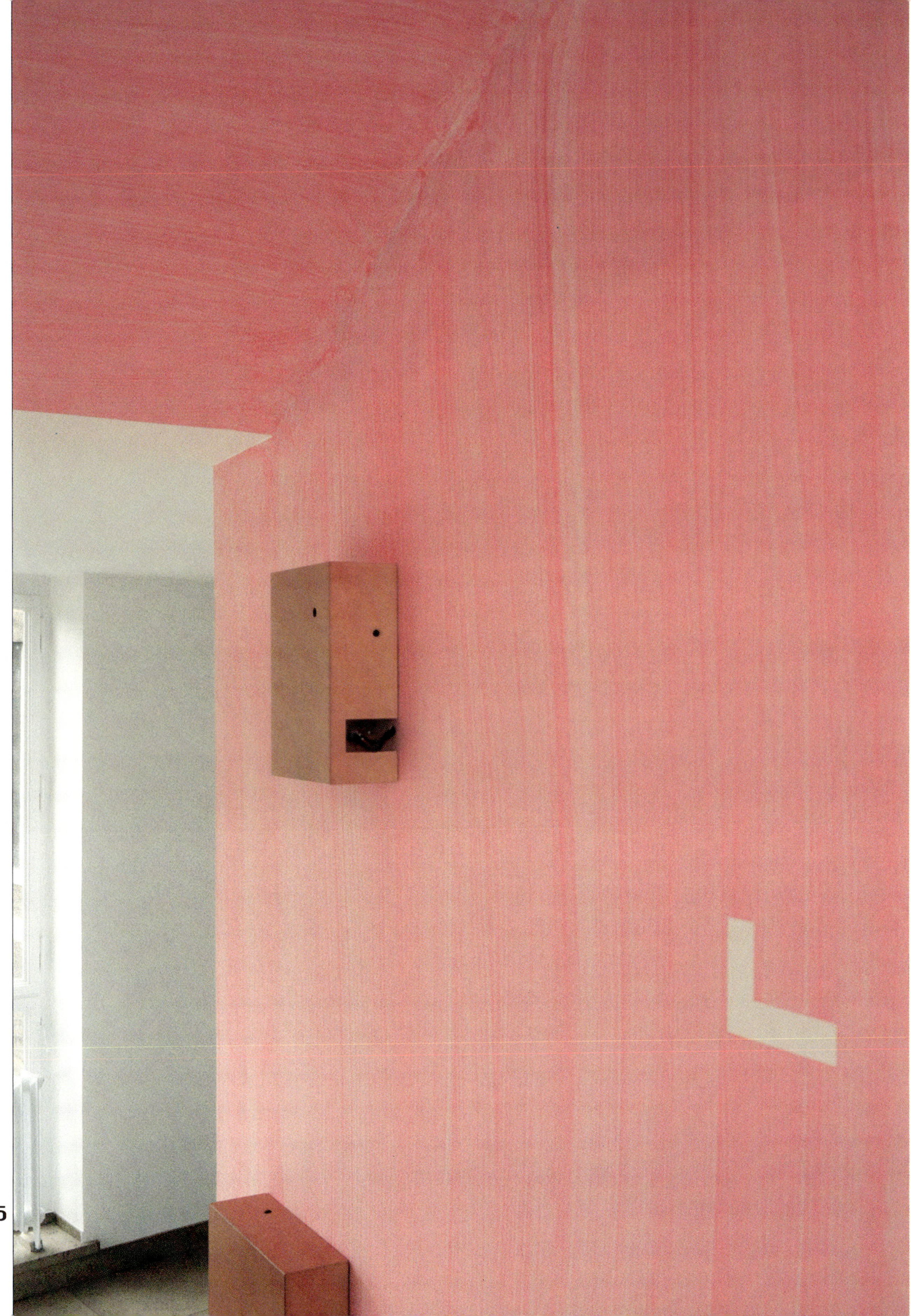

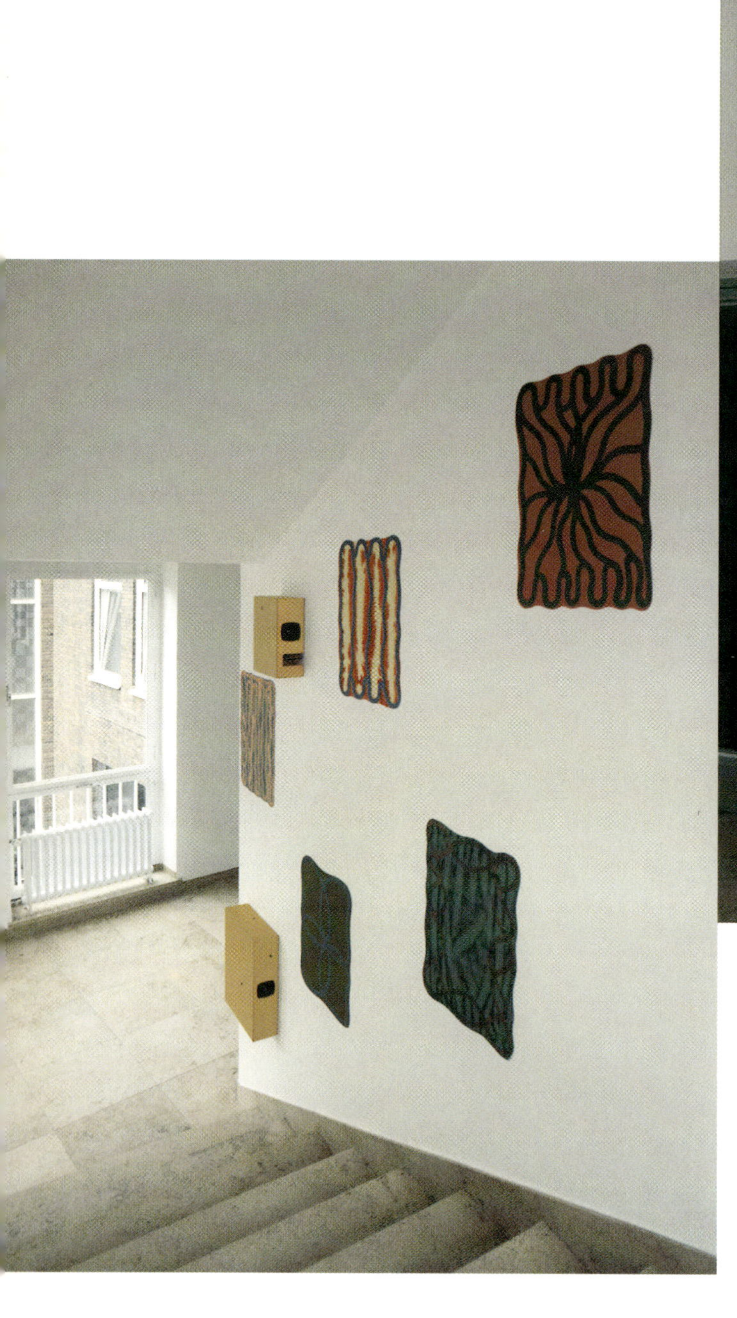

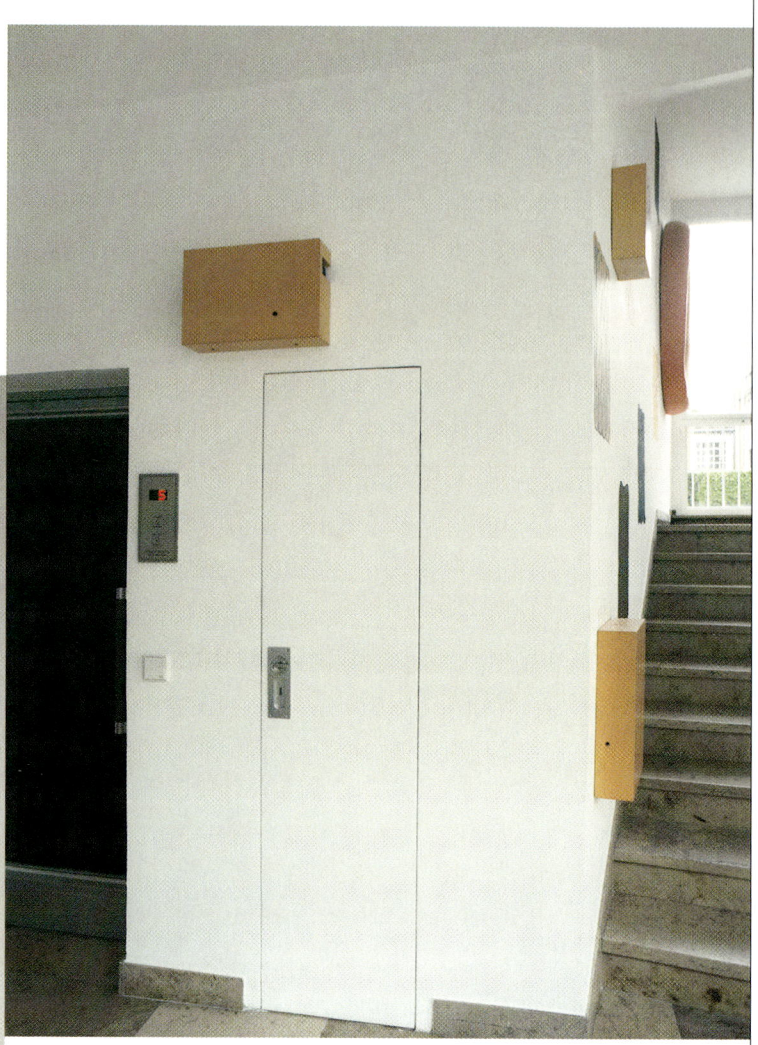

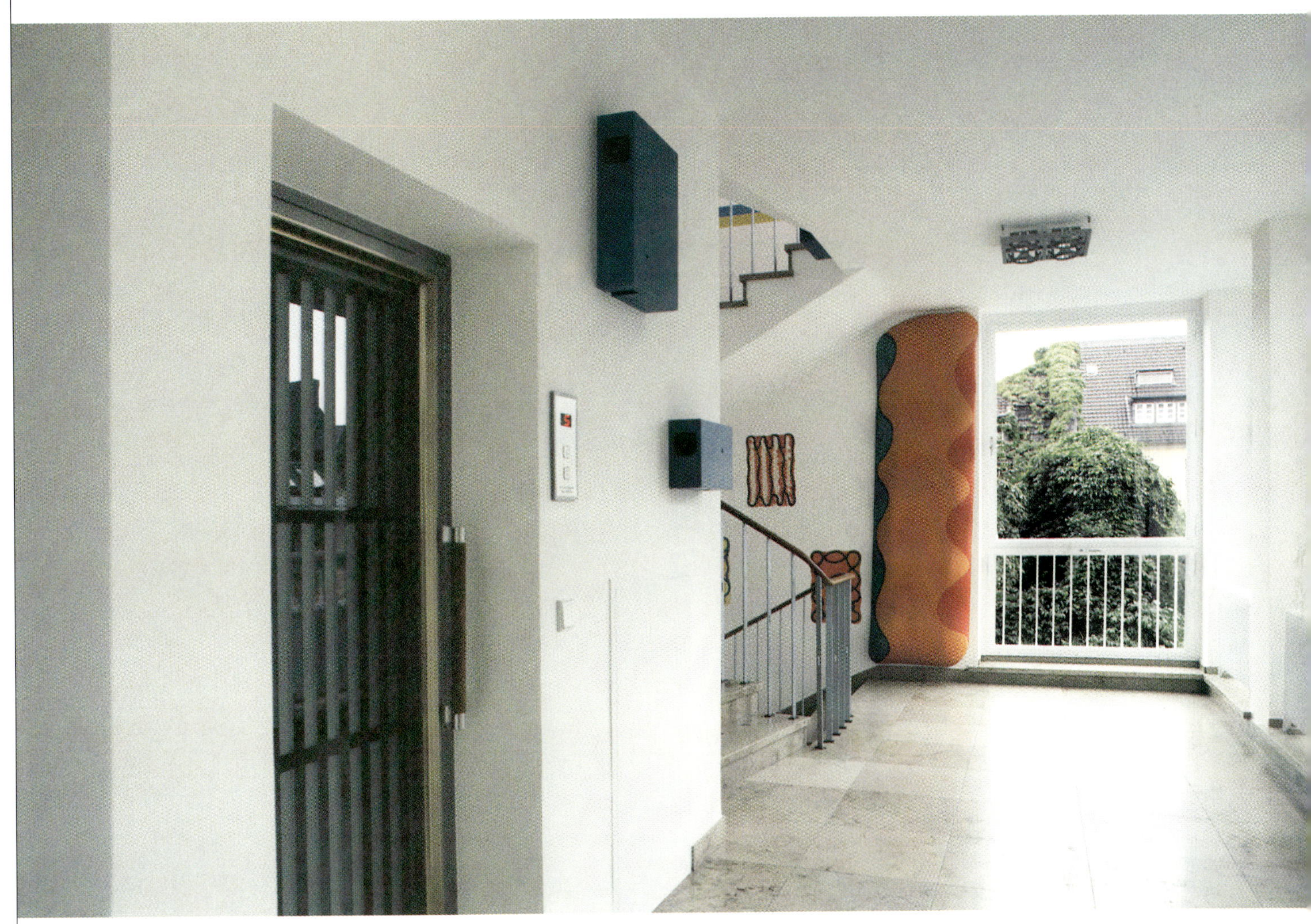

Die grundlegende Idee war, einen Klang-Begleiter zu bauen – ein zigarettenschachtelgroßes Gerät, das man überall hin mitnehmen kann und das – je nach ausgewähltem Programm – Umweltgeräusche in parallele klangliche Strukturen umwandelt. Als ein Prototyp für dieses vermarktbare kleine Gerät wurde 1997 der semi-stationäre Transformer entwickelt (zwar batteriebetrieben aber immer noch relativ groß...). In einer Auflage von 10 Stück gebaut, transferiert er die Erfahrungen, die während des Kunitachi Projekts gewonnen wurden, in eine Programmierung, die flexibel auf sich verändernde Eingaben reagieren kann – zum Beispiel wechselt es nach einer bestimmten Anzahl von Wiederholungen die Programm-Stufe oder Differenzierung.

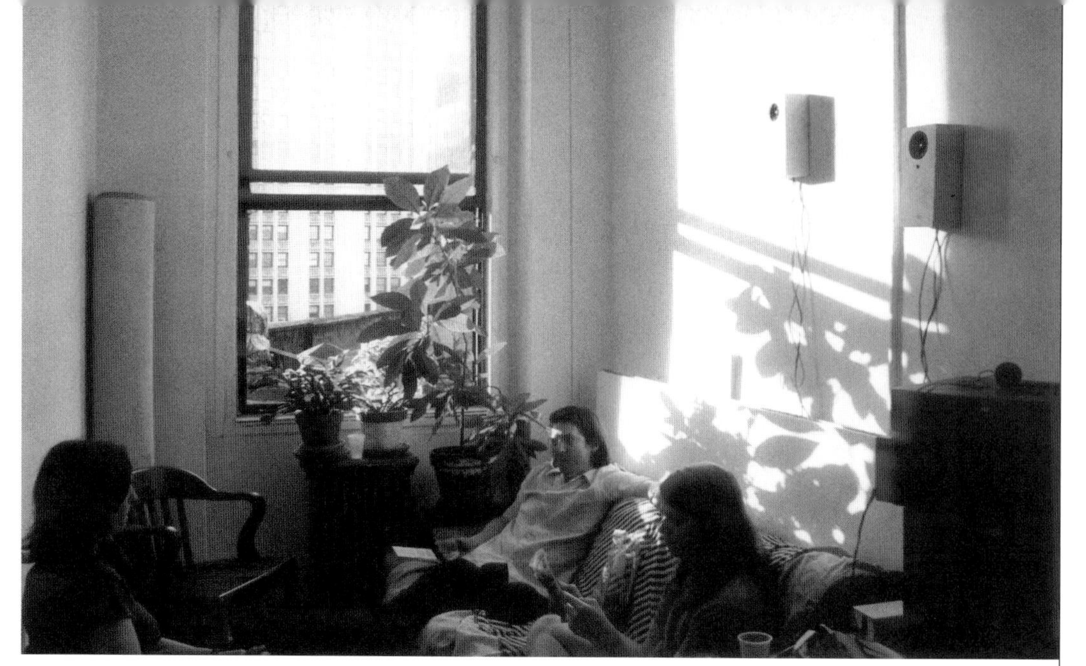

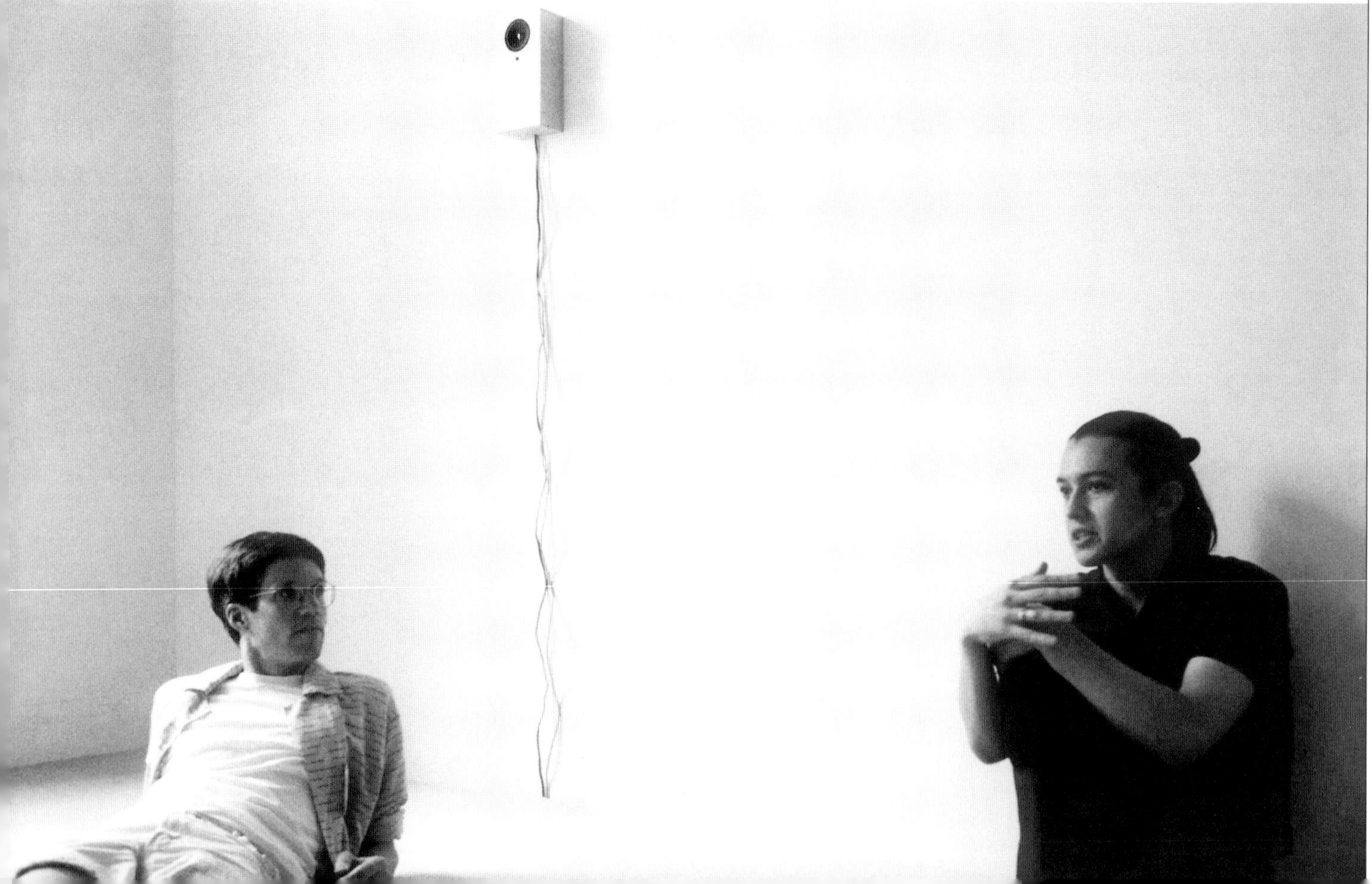

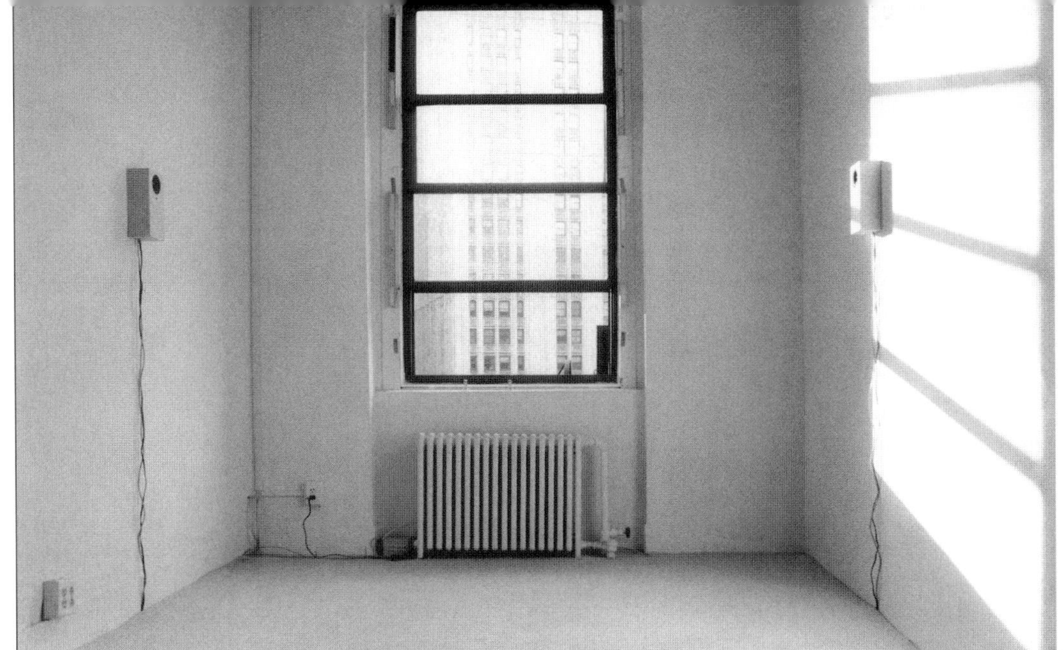

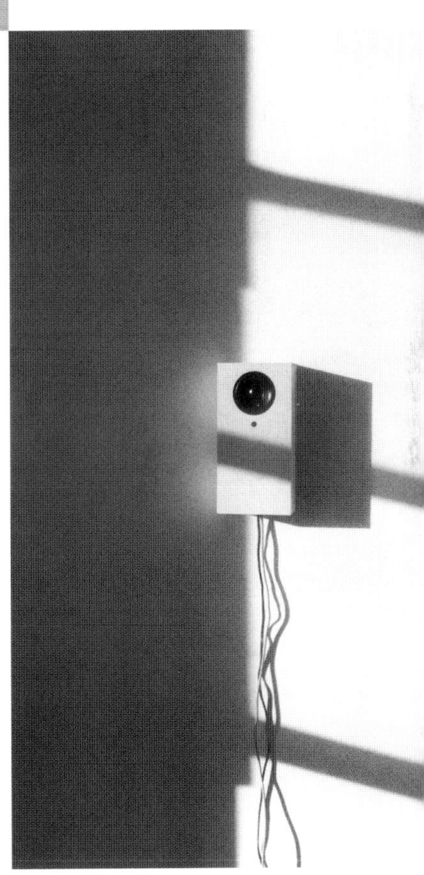

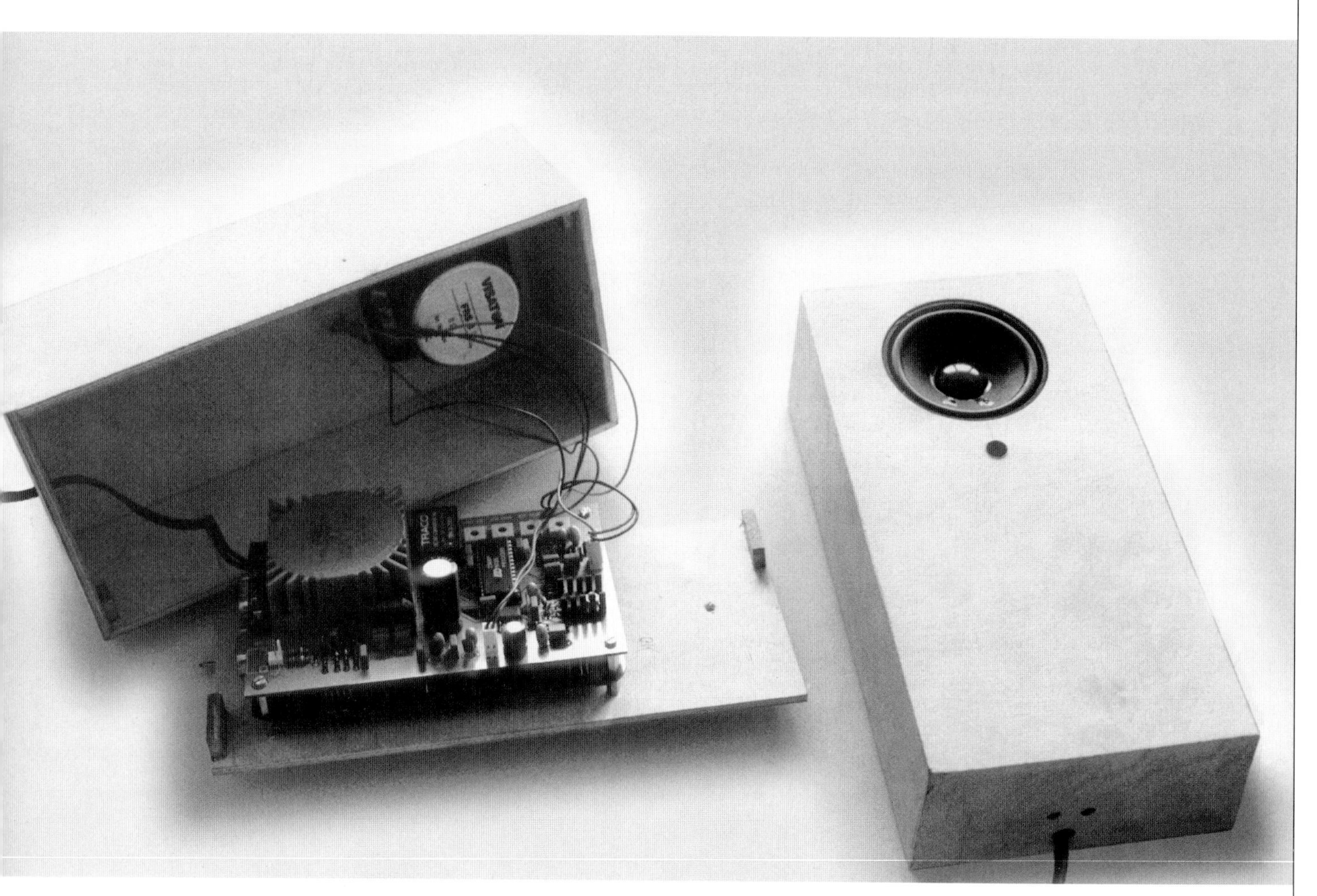

"**Connective memory**" is situated in the recess hall of a secondary school where it scans the sound profile of the students' voices. According to compositional patterns, certain sonic forms are selected, recorded and stored in digital memory. If a discernible sound event takes place, the memory adds a related sound formation to the live sound. While the system is at work, the red squares on the ceiling of the recess hall are lit. At the same time the outside "checkerboard" light-square translates the sonic impulse into a game of moving lights. Composition is thus conceived as an interrelated system of "filters": compositional density (or openness...) results from the listeners' participation and the modesby which they preconceive relatedness. The system is open in two respects: via modem the computer is remote-controlled, thus the program can be adjusted to possible changes in the profile of sonic communication at any time. As part of an educational program the pupils are also introduced to the basic features of the program and can work out their personal light pattern/movement which will be on display until the next student's program is installed...

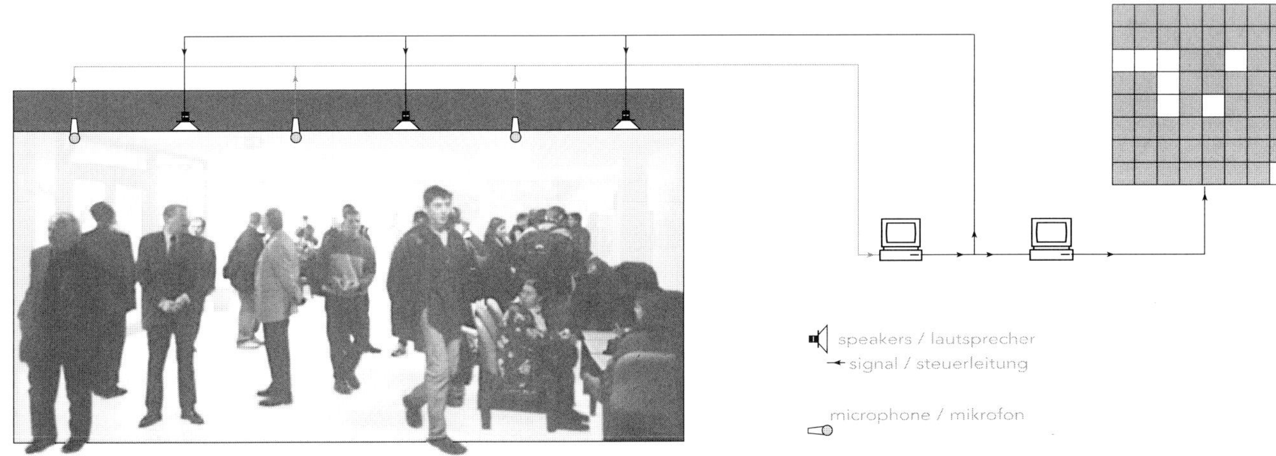

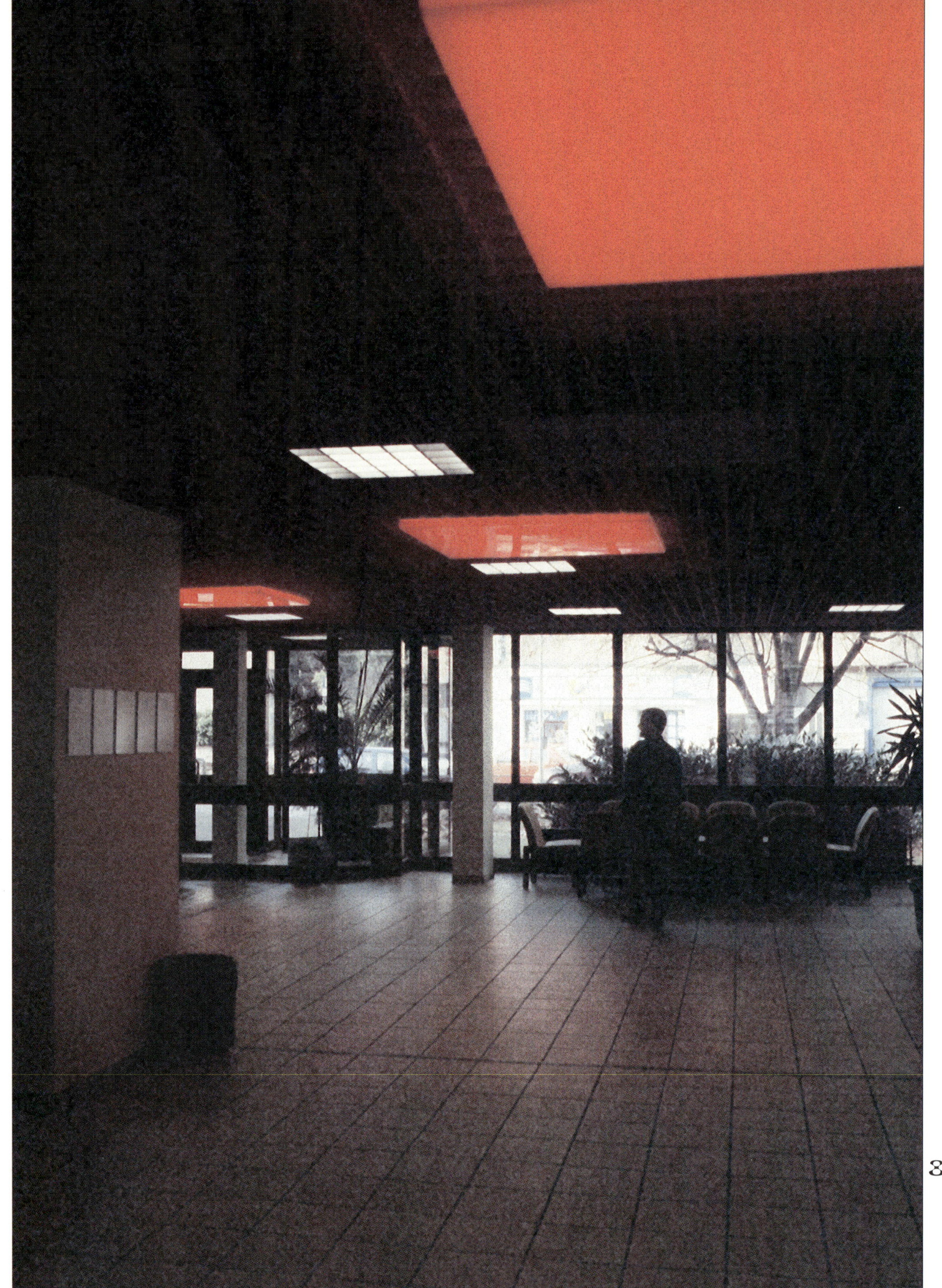

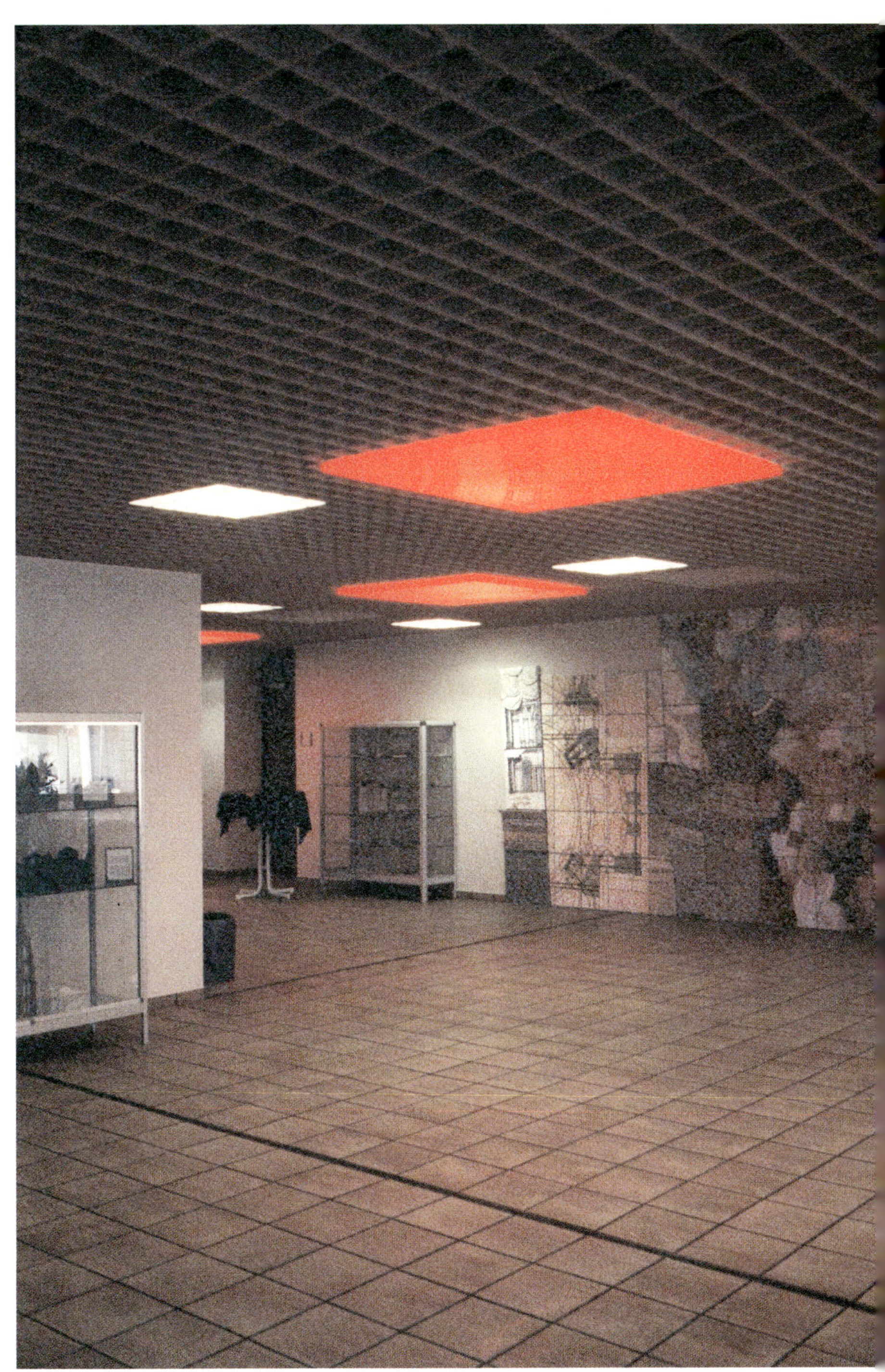

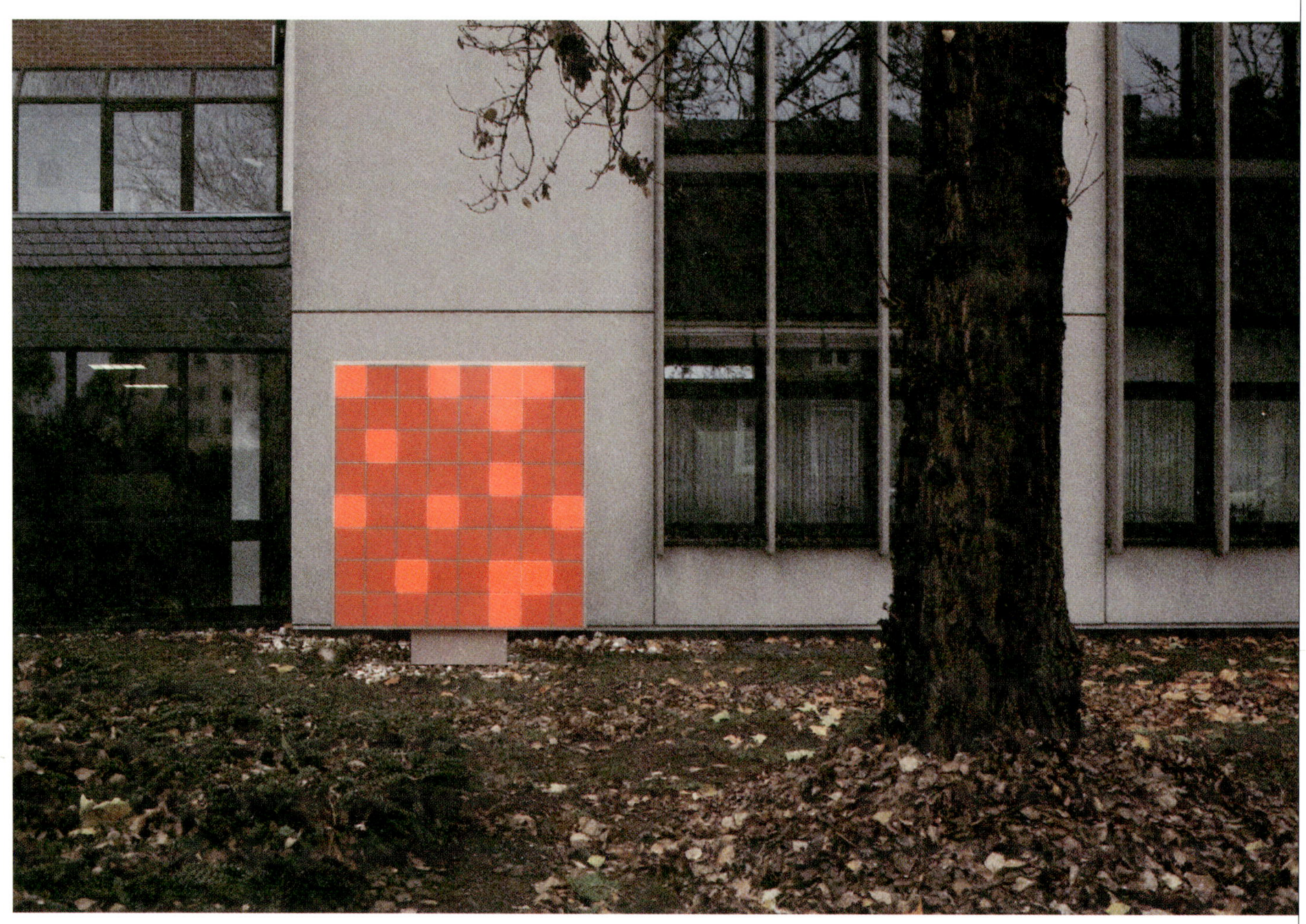

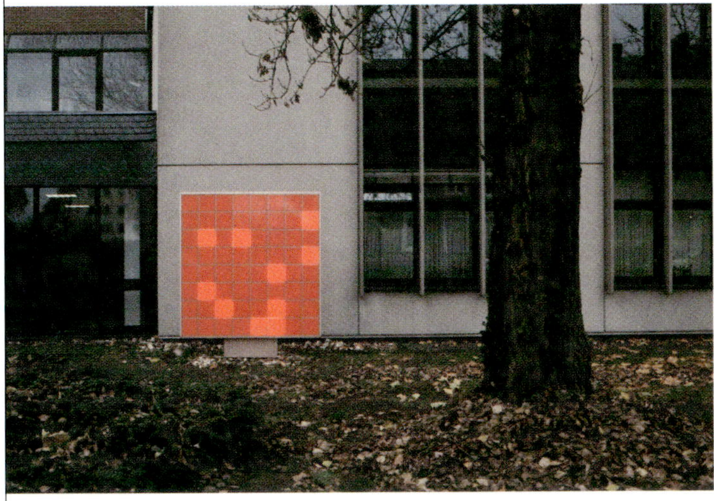

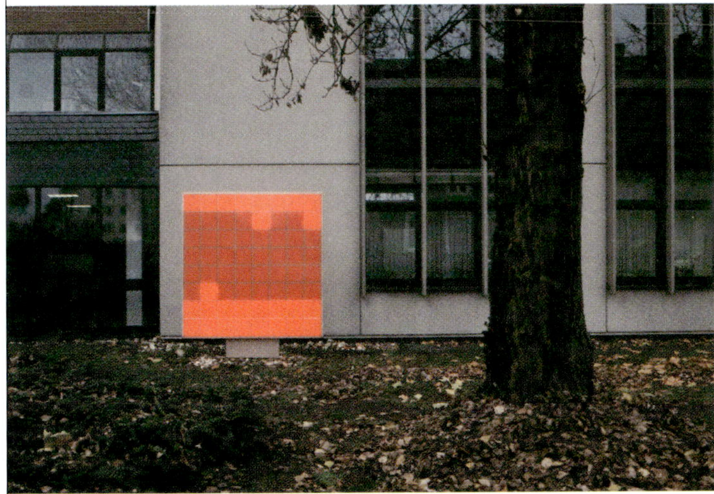

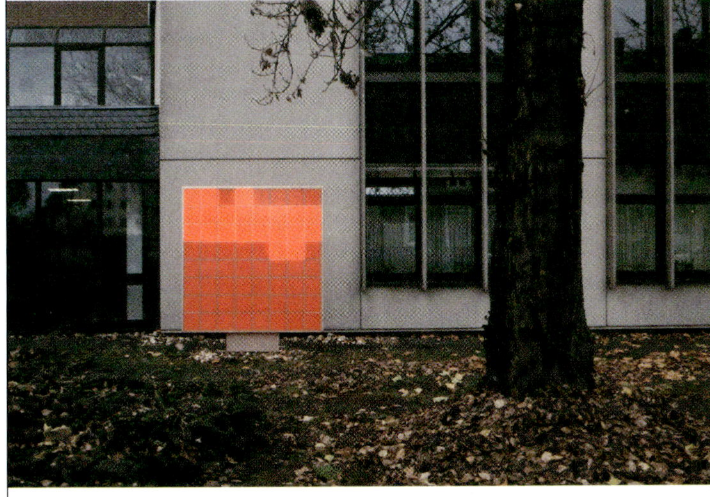

„Connective memory" befindet sich in der Pausenhalle eines Gymnasiums, in der es die Klang-Profile der Schülerstimmen aufnimmt und analysiert. Nach kompositorischen Vorgaben werden bestimmte klangliche Formen ausgewählt, aufgezeichnet und in einem digitalen Speicher aufbewahrt. Wenn ein konturiertes Klangereignis stattfindet, fügt „Connective memory" dem live-sound eine vergleichbare Klangformation aus dem Speicher bei. Solange das System angeschaltet ist, sind die roten Deckenfelder beleuchtet. Gleichzeitig ist auf dem Licht-Schachbrett vor der Schule eine Übersetzung der Klang-Formationen in Licht-Bewegung zu sehen.

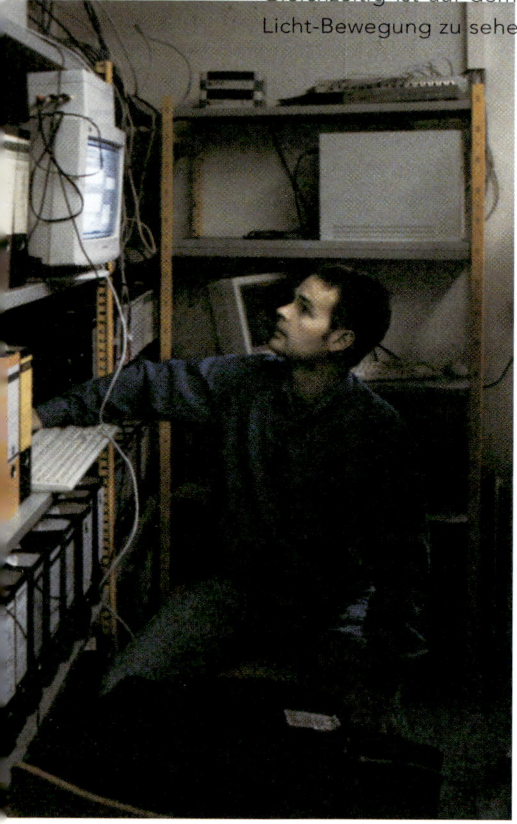

Komposition erstellt so einer Reihe untereinander verbundener Filter: kompositorische Dichte (oder Offenheit...) resultiert aus der Teilnahme der Hörer und der Art und Weise, in der sie Verbindung vorvollziehen. Das System ist offen in zweifacher Hinsicht: es ist mittels Modem fernsteuerbar – so kann das Programm an mögliche Veränderungen im Profil der Klang-Kommunikation angepasst werden. Und als Teil der Lehre werden Schüler mit den grundsätzlichen Funktionen des Programms bekannt gemacht und können – im Rahmen von Kursen – die Art und Weise bestimmen, in der die Transformation von Klang in Licht-Bewegung stattfindet.

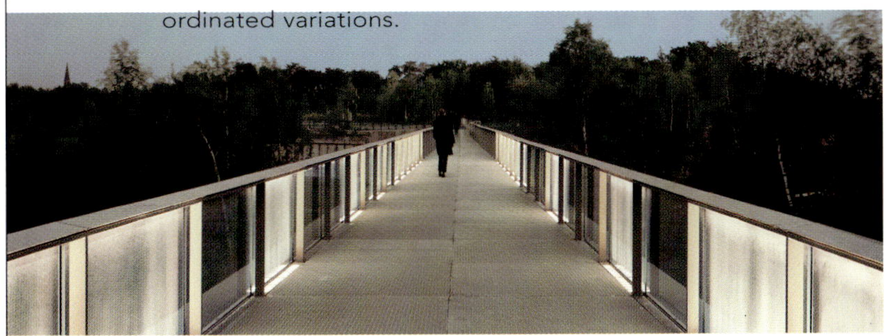

The bridge, a 80 m long steel construction, has spanned the entrance to the old Krupp steel-plant in Bochum, Germany, since September 1999. The artwork which was conceived and developed simultaneous to the planning and construction of the bridge, consists of a (reflecting) glass railing and a lighting system which can light the 126 single panes independently. Depending on the motion of the people on the bridge, which is recorded by 26 radar detection systems, the light moves along with the pedestrians' movements –– moreover an additional composition creates light patterns that connect the basic movement with systems of co-ordinated variations.

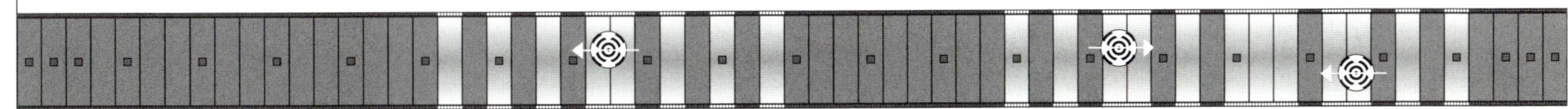

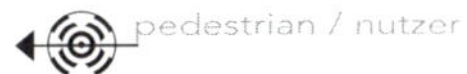

halogen unit / strahler

sensors / sensoren

pedestrian / nutzer

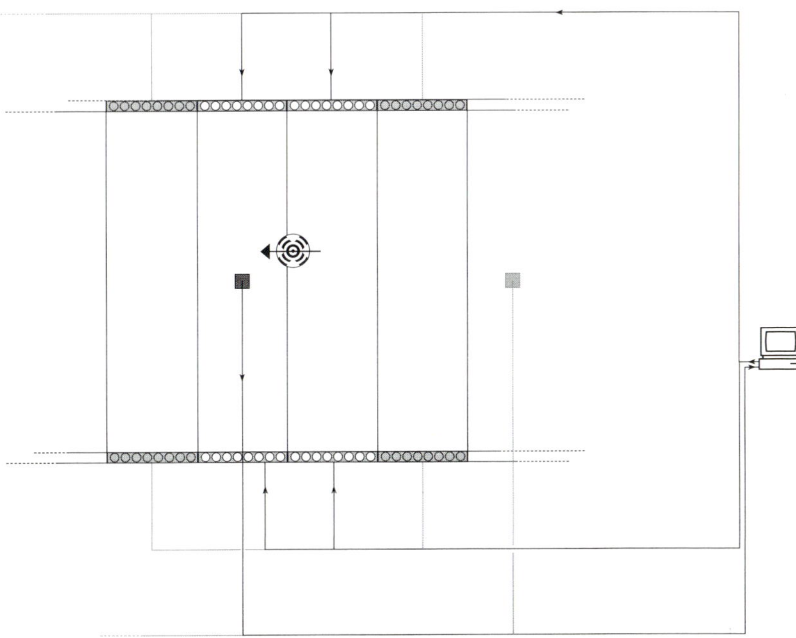

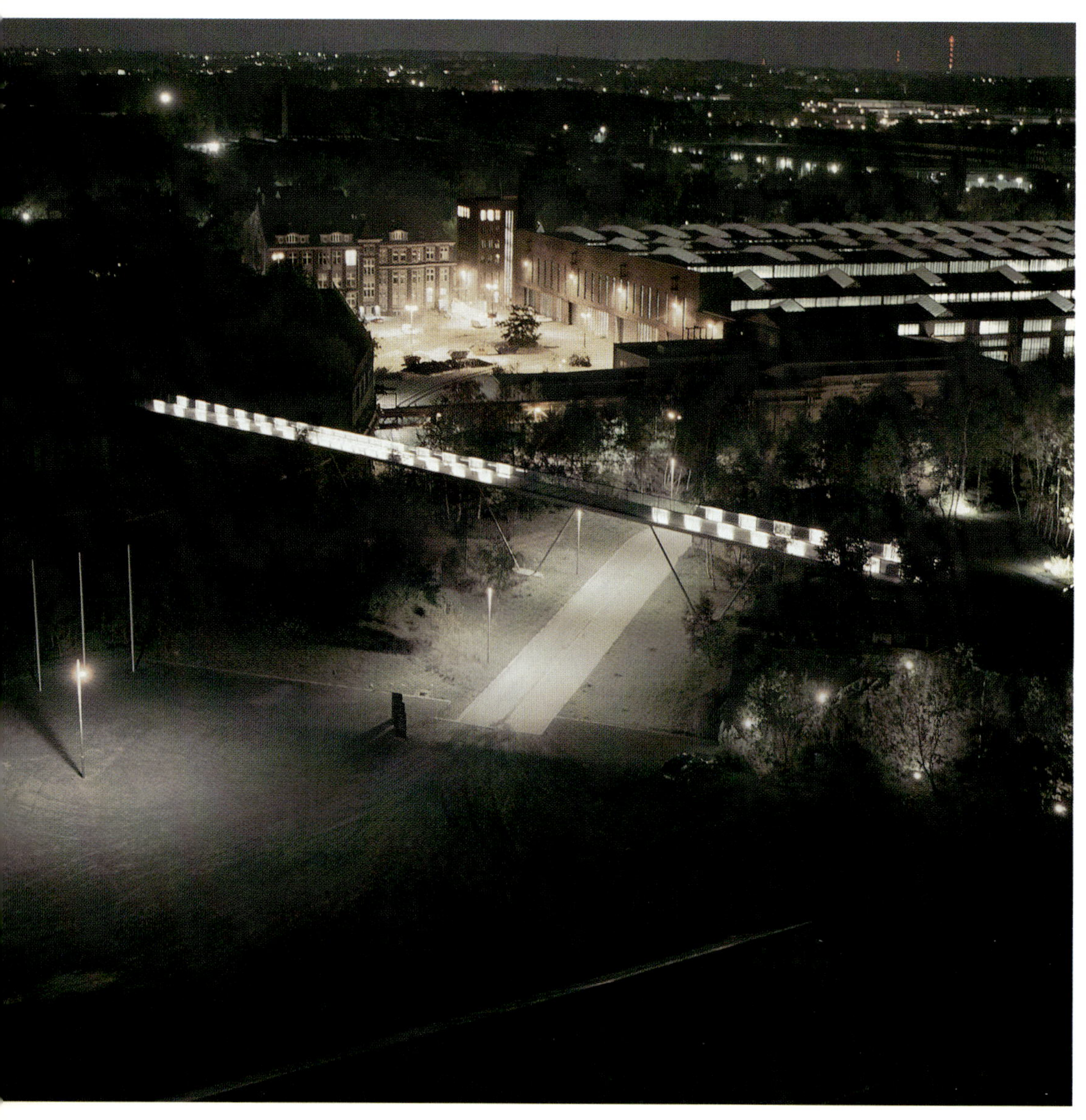

Die Brücke, eine 80 m lange Stahl-Konstruktion, überspannt den Eingang zum früheren Krupp Stahlwerk in Bochum. Das künstlerische Projekt, das zeitgleich mit Planung und Bau der Brücke entwickelt und realisiert wurde, besteht aus dem Licht-reflektierenden Glas-Geländer und einem Licht-System, das es ermöglicht, die 126 Scheiben des Geländers einzeln anzustrahlen. Parallel zu den Bewegungen der Fußgänger auf der Brücke, die von kleinen Radar-Systemen aufgezeichnet werden, bewegt sich das Licht: jede Person hat ihre eigene Korona. Zusätzlich erzeugt eine Komposition Licht-Patterns, die die Grundbewegung durch ein System koordinierter Variationen ergänzt.

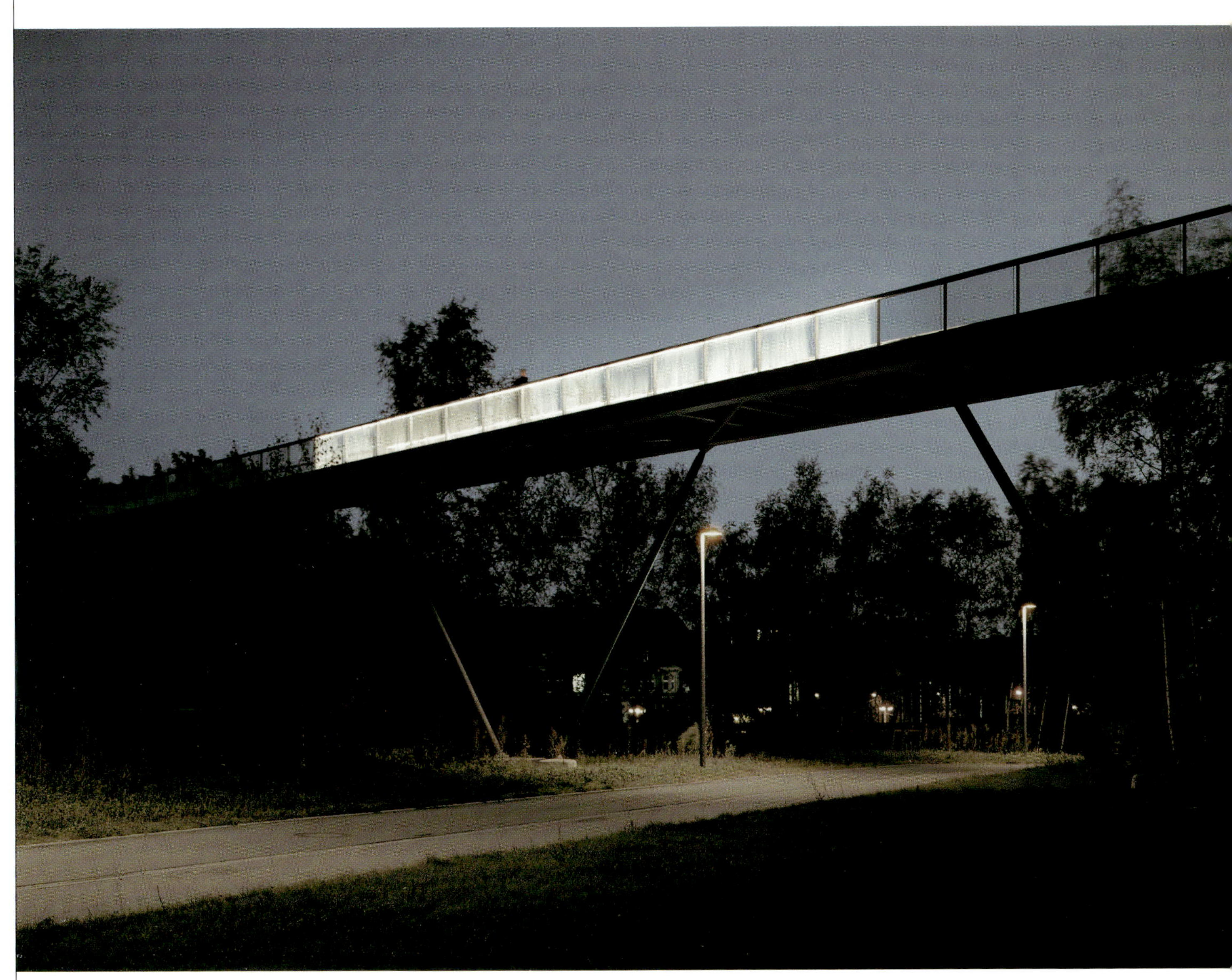

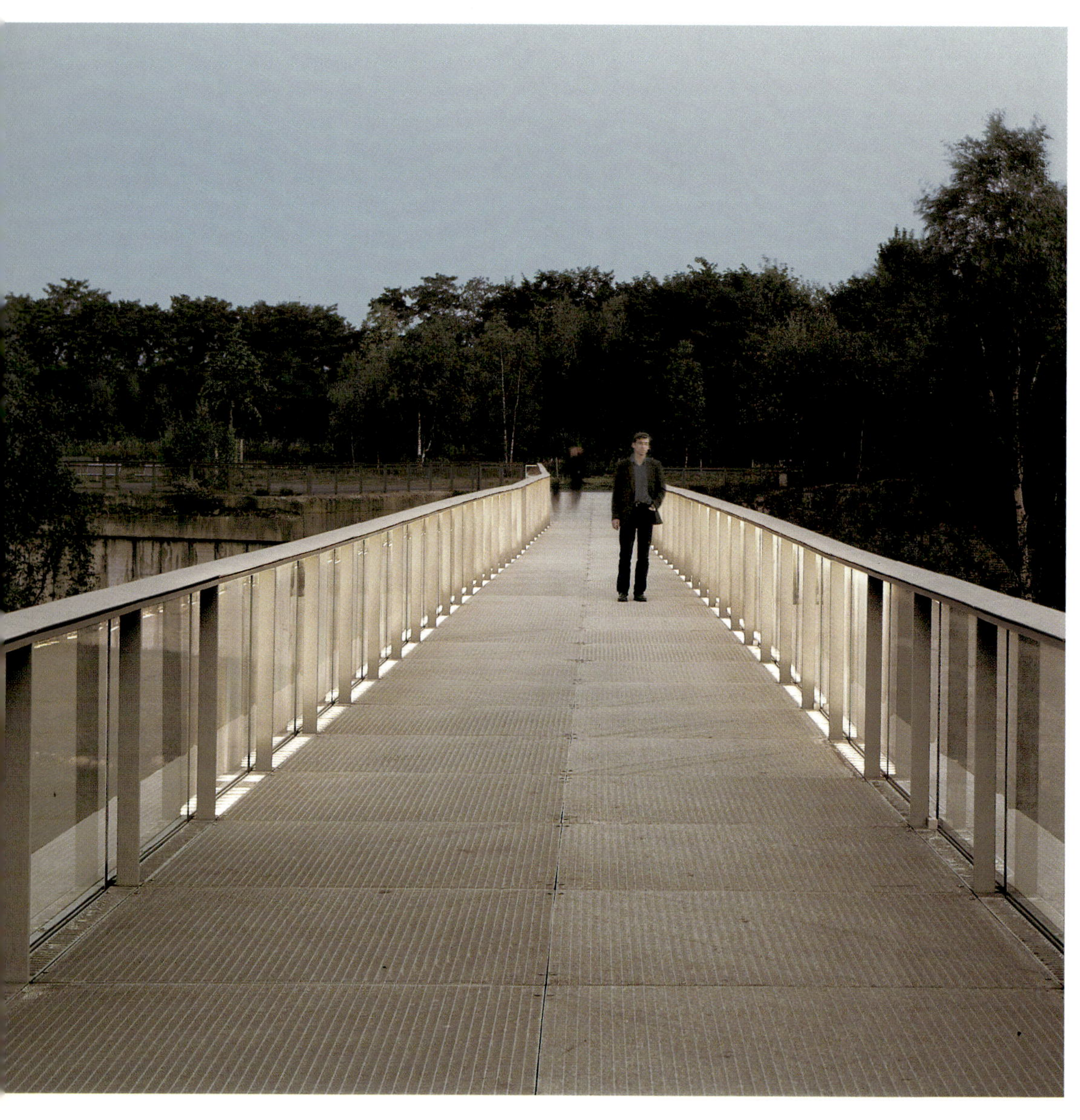

Three walls in a house (designed by the Frankfurt based architects Seifert/Stöckmann), that can be turned on like a stereo. The sounds one will hear are the (real-time) outside noises –– processed and transformed. The system can be switched to reverse mode: inside noise can be projected to the outside as well.

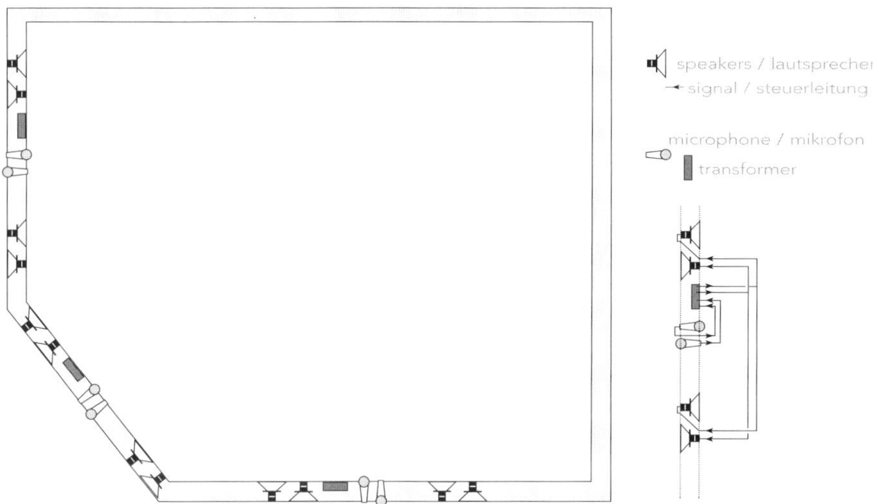

3 Wände des Hauses (gebaut von Seifert/Stöckmann Architekten) können wie eine Stereo-Anlage angeschaltet werden. Die Klangereignisse, die innen zu hören sind, sind die tatsächlich draußen stattfindenden – allerdings verrechnet und transformiert – d.h. je nach Bedarf stark oder schwach abstrahiert. Das System funktioniert auch in umgekehrter Richtung: die Innen-Geräusche werden dann, je nach Wunsch und Auswahl des Nutzers mehr oder weniger verändert, nach außen projiziert.

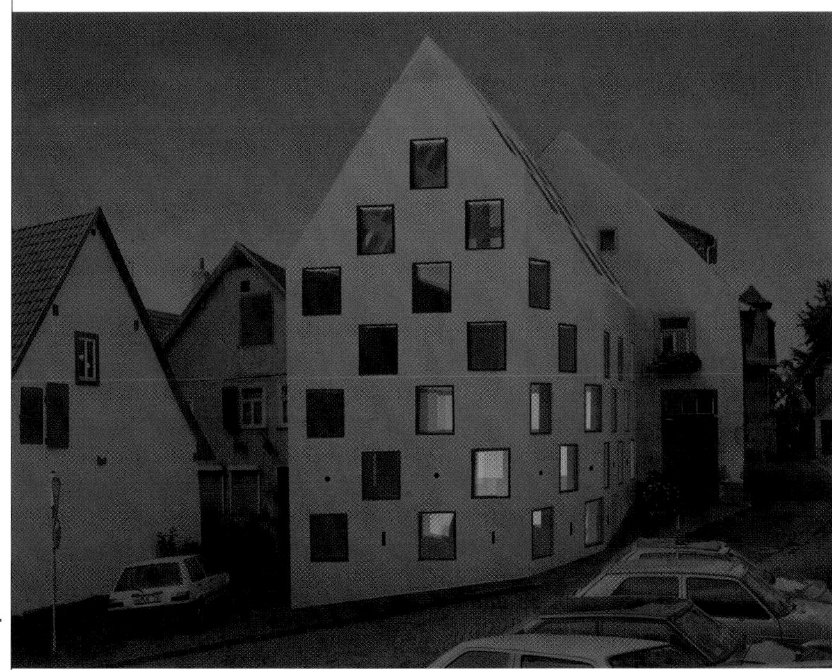

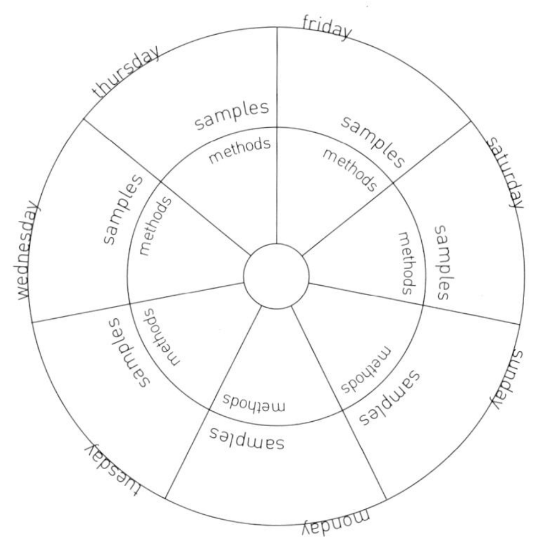

friday
thursday
wednesday
tuesday
monday
sunday
saturday
samples
methods
samples
methods
samples
methods
samples
methods
samples
methods
samples
methods
samples
methods

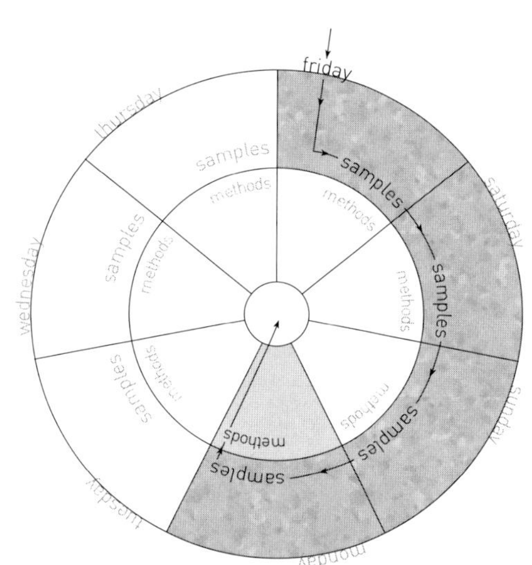

friday
thursday
wednesday
tuesday
monday
sunday
saturday
samples
methods
samples
methods
samples
methods
samples
methods
samples
methods
samples
methods
samples
methods

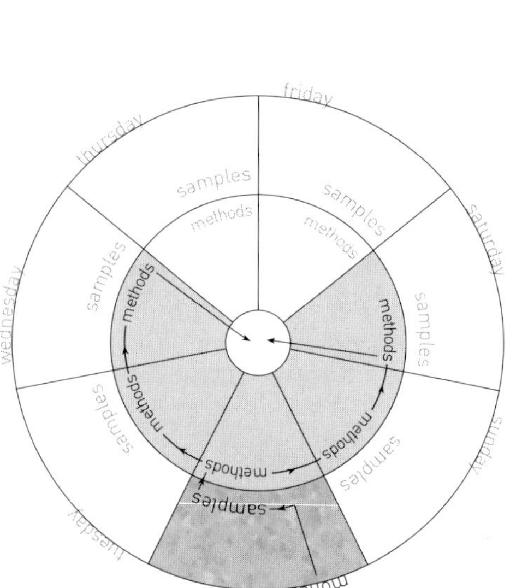

friday
thursday
wednesday
tuesday
monday
sunday
saturday
samples
methods
samples
methods
samples
methods
samples
methods
samples
methods
samples
methods
samples
methods

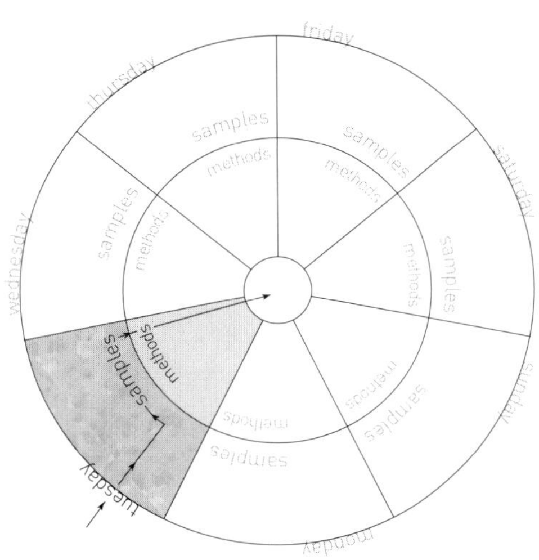

Nach dem Deutschen Rundfunk-Gesetz hat das (nicht-kommerzielle) Frankfurter „RadioX" eine bestimmte Summe als GEMA-Abgabe zu entrichten. Um die Summe zu verringern, wird die Nacht-Schiene mit GEMA-freier Musik bespielt. Deshalb entwerfen die ...imaginary soundscapes... für diese Nachtschiene eine offene Struktur, die die Kombination von Klangmaterial in steter Bewegung hält. Jeder der (idealerweise sieben) beteiligten Künstler/Komponisten hat seinen entsprechenden Wochentag (bzw. Nacht) und eine Sektion auf der Festplatte: diese unterteilt sich in 2 Abschnitte – die eine enthält Samples (d.h. Klänge und Klangmaterialien) und die andere Methoden (die kompositorischen Regeln, die die Modifikation der Sample-Kombinationen definieren). Jeder Komponist kann den Zugang zu seinen Samples und Methoden erlauben, so daß z.B. „Montag" die Methoden von „Mittwoch" benutzt, um die Samples von „Samstag" und „Sonntag" zu bearbeiten.

SLP ...p.45
(a SELEKTION project)

Performances: ICMC, Köln ,1988; Ferienkurse für Neue Musik,
Darmstadt, 1988; Leipziger Jazz-Tage, 1989; Art Frankfurt, 1990; Ars
Electronica, Linz, 1990; Festival für Experimentelle Musik, München,
1991

Photos: Markus Caspers, AW

Mixer ...p.39
2 nights in 1992

Technical support: Jürgen Brendel,
Dietmar Grau
Organisation: Andreas Kallfelz

Photos: AW

Futur Interieur ...p.41
Nancy, France, 1993
festival organisation: Denis Paris

Sine-sound generators: Jürgen Brendel
Steelworks: Ferdinand Rose
Support: Gilla Lörcher

Photos: AW

Oppositionen und Schwesterfelder ...p.54
an exhibition at Sezession, Vienna 1993
Organisation: Sabine B. Vogel

Hardware and interface: Jürgen Brendel

Photos: AW

Lahnstrasse
installed from 1993 until 2000 at top floor, Lahnstrasse 37, Frankfurt a.M.

Hardware: Jürgen Brendel
Light-elements: Daniel Zerlang-Roesch

Photos: Meyer und Kunz

BZF
Installed permanently at the "Behördenzentrum Frankfurt" since 1993
(Gutleutstrasse 116 - 124, Frankfurt a.M.)

Hardware: TEBA
Technical support: Luigi Cavallera

Photos: Meyer und Kunz

rot/2rot
(rot: 1994, 2rot: 1995)

a collaboration with Manfred H. Wenninger

rot actresses: Kattrin Deufert
                      Regina Brown
                      Ruth Schlagbauer
                      Susanne Eggert

Sine-sound generators, light-interface: Jürgen Brendel
Technical support: Marcus Brown

2rot actresses: Kattrin Deufert
                      Regina Brown
                      Ruth Schlagbauer
                      Beate Maurer
                      Katharina Grosch-Wackernagel
                      Sonja Hilke
Sonja Rode
Stefanie Schander

Hardware, sound: TEBA
Hardware, light: Jürgen Brendel

Photos: Charly Steiger

Clappers ...p.60
(documented on the "moves"- CD, SELEKTION, SCD 020, 1996)

Hardware, sound: TEBA
Software: Ulrich Habfast

Performances:
"sonic perception", Kawasaki City Museum, 1995
Musikhochschule Frankfurt, 1996
Gallery Insect, Boston, 1997
Anomalous, Seattle, 1997
The Lab, San Francisco, 1997
"KORZO", Den Haag, 1997

the rebuilt, interactive version:

Beyond Music Festival, Los Angeles, 2000
Studio 5 Beekman, New York, 2000

Photos: AW

Kunitachi sound transformation ...p.64
Kunitachi (Tokyo), 1996

Hardware by TEBA
Software: Dirk Witschke
Support: Kaname Oda

(special thanks to Gallery KIGOMA, Kunitachi; Kawasaki City Museum,
Kawasaki; Goethe-Institut, Tokyo; Motorola Germany)

Photos: Atsushi Tominaga, AW

staircase window ...p.68
Haus Steiger, Langen/Hessen, realized 1996/97.

Light System: Daniel Zerlang-Roesch
Software: Jürgen Brendel, Volker Abel
Hardware: TEBA
Glass: BGT
Steelworks: Werner Horn

Photos: Meyer und Kunz

wall-field ...p.91
Installed permanently, Kuhgasse 15, Gelnhausen, Germany
Architects: Gabriela Seifert, Götz Stöckmann

Hardware: TEBA
Software: Dirk Witschke

Photos: Charly Steiger

Transformer ...p.74

Hardware by TEBA
Sound-programming: Dirk Witschke

the transformers were shown at:
"relocations", Mainz, 1997
studio 5 Beekman, New York, 1997
INM, Frankfurt a.M., 1999
"living room", AA (Architectural Assosiation) , London, 1999

10 transformers are permanently installed at Droege & comp. Poststrasse 4-6,
Düsseldorf
(Special thanks to Kaegi Projects)

Some versions of the transformer programs are on "acts" SELEKTION, SCD 026,
1998

Photos: AW

Light-net ...p.70
Collaboration with INDEX Planungsgruppe (Sigrun Musa + Ulrich Exner)
installed permanently at Fachhochschule (Technical University) Frankfurt a.M.
since 1998

Hardware: TEBA
Software and sound-programming: Dirk Witschke
Support: Luigi Cavallera

Photos: Meyer und Kunz

Nordpol-Brücke …p.87
installed permanently at City West Park, Bochum since summer 2000.

Hardware: TEBA
Software: MESO (Sebastian Oschatz), Dirk Witschke
Glass: BGT
Light: Inprotec
Light consultant: Daniel Zerlang-Roesch
Architects: Hegger, Hegger, Schleif;
Bollinger und Grohmann

Photos: Constantin Meyer

connective memory …p.81
Installed permanently at Balthasar Neumann Technikum, Trier,
Germany since 1999.

Light-system: Nordlicht
Software: Volker Abel
Support: Hartmut Friedel

Photos: AW

Radio X …p.92
instigated by Petra Ilyes

a collaboration project with
Dirk Witschke
Karl Kliem
Peter Fey

concept: AW

Wollscheid's office (1997) …p.95
3. Welt-Haus-Chor, Frankfurt a.M., rehearsing